The Mediterranean Diet Cookbook for Beginners

2000 Days of Tantalizing and Effortless Recipes with a 28-Day Meal Plan to Ignite Your Health and Palate

Sandra H. Herrington

Copyright© 2023 By Sandra H. Herrington Rights Reserved

This book is copyright protected. It is only for personal use. You cannot amend, distribute, sell, use, quote or paraphrase any part of the content within this book, without the consent of the author or publisher.

Under no circumstances will any blame or legal responsibility be held against the publisher, or author, for any damages, reparation, or monetary loss due to the information contained within this book, either directly or indirectly.

Disclaimer Notice:

Please note the information contained within this document is for educational and entertainment purposes only. All effort has been executed to present accurate, up to date, reliable, complete information. No warranties of any kind are declared or implied. Readers acknowledge that the author is not engaged in the rendering of legal, financial, medical or professional advice. The content within this book has been derived from various sources. Please consult a licensed professional before attempting any techniques outlined in this book.

By reading this document, the reader agrees that under no circumstances is the author responsible for any losses, direct or indirect, that are incurred as a result of the use of the information contained within this document, including, but not limited to, errors, omissions, or inaccuracies.

Editor: AALIYAH LYONS

Interior Design: BROOKE WHITE

Cover Art: DANIELLE REES

Food stylist: SIENNA ADAMS

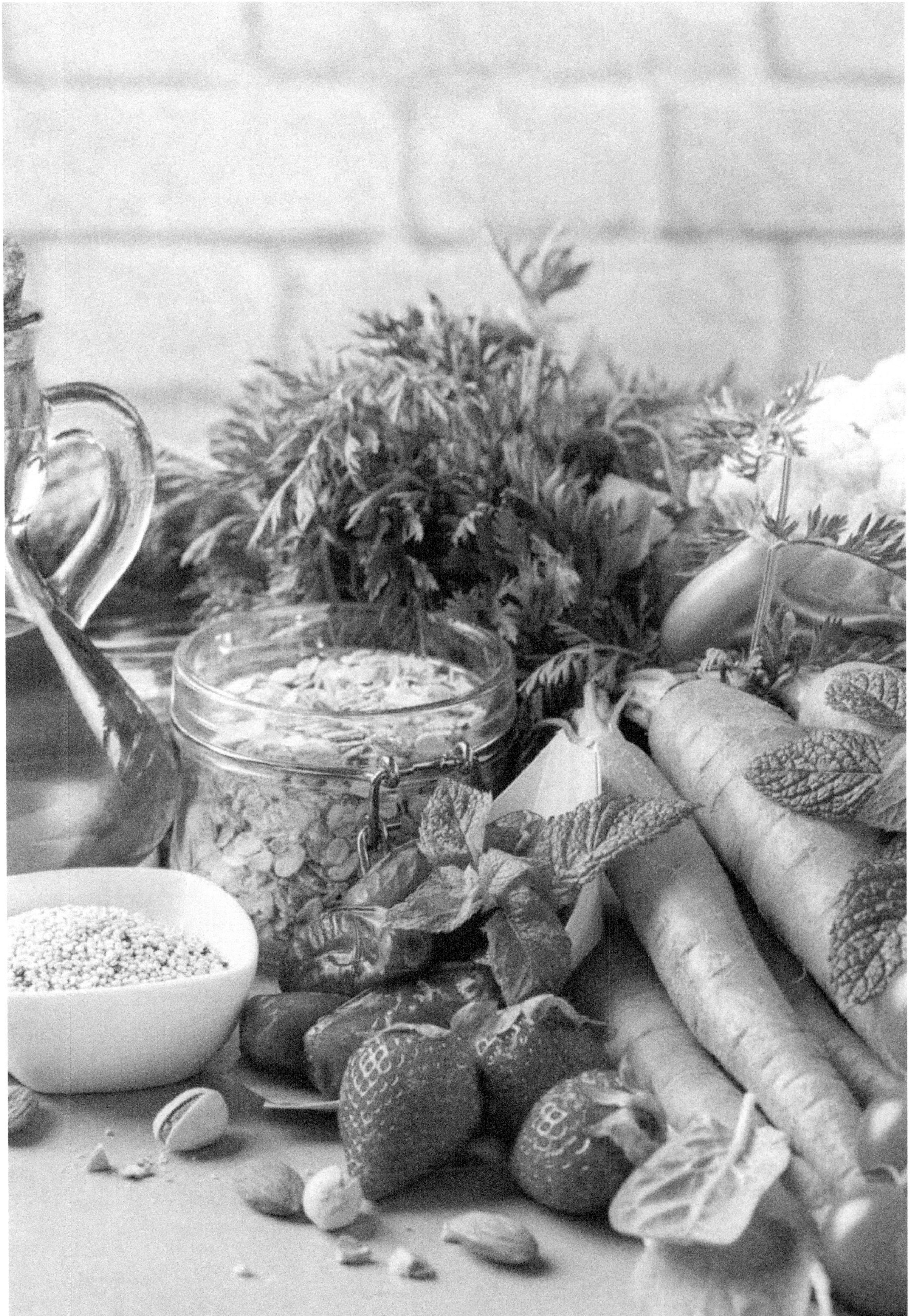

Table Of Contents

Introduction	1	Secrets	12
		Shopping List for Week 3	12
Chapter 1		Week 4: Celebrating Your Transformative	
Embracing a Mediterranean Lifestyle	2	Journey	13
Historical and Cultural Significance	3	Shopping List for Week 4	13
Benefits of the Mediterranean Diet	4		
Stocking Your Mediterranean Pantry	7	**Chapter 3**	
		Breakfast and Brunch	14
Chapter 2		Ratatouille with Poached Eggs	15
28-Day Meal Plan	9	Israeli Eggplant and Egg Sandwiches	15
Week 1: Embracing the Mediterranean		Garlic & Bell Pepper Frittata	16
Diet	10	Caprese Scrambled Eggs	16
Shopping List for Week 1	10	Carrot Bread	16
Week 2: Diving Deeper into Mediterranean		Italian Ricotta & Tomato Omelet	17
Delights	11	Scrambled Eggs with Feta and Olives	17
Shopping List for Week 2	11	Cauliflower Pizza Crusts	17
Week 3: Unleashing the Mediterranean		Cranberry Bread	18

Dilled Tuna Salad Sandwich	18
Peachy Green Smoothie	18
Fried Eggs with Potato and Parmesan Pancake	19
Spanish Tortilla with Roasted Red Peppers	20
Honey and Avocado Smoothie	20
Peach and Walnut Breakfast Salad	21
Thin-Crust Pizza	21
Scrambled Eggs with Prosciutto	22
Scrambled Eggs with Potatoes and Harissa	22
Za'atar Bread	23
Savory Breakfast Oats	23
Scrambled Eggs with Piperade	24
Broccoli and Feta Frittata	24

Chapter 4
Soups and Small Plates — 25

Old-Fashioned Chicken Soup	26
Rustic Winter Salad	26
Yellow and White Hearts of Palm Salad	26
Asparagus Salad	26
Chorizo Sausage & Fire-Roasted Tomato Soup	27
Mushroom and Potato Stew	27
Novara's Bean and Vegetable Soup	28
Creamy Asparagus Soup	28
Sautéed Scallops with Garlic and Parsley	29
Tomato and Pepper Salad	29
Herby Tomato Soup	30
White Bean and Kale Soup	30
Fig-Pecan Energy Bites	30
Hard-Boiled Eggs with Green Sauce	31
Parsley Garden Vegetable Soup	31
Double-Apple Spinach Salad	31
Riviera Tuna Salad	32
Lamb & Spinach Soup	32

Chapter 5
Rice, Grains and Pasta — 33

Wild Rice and Kale Stuffed Chicken Thighs	34
Spanish-Style Brothy Rice with Clams and Salsa Verde	34
Toasted Grain and Almond Pilaf	35
Indoor Paella	35
Easy Spanish Rice	36
Beef-Stuffed Pasta Shells	36
Sautéed Cherry Tomato and Fresh Mozzarella Topping	36
Mediterranean Lentils and Rice	37
Pasta Caprese Ricotta-Basil Fusilli	37
Lebanese Rice and Broken Noodles with Cabbage	38
Grilled Paella	38
Creamy Parmesan Polenta	39
Chili-Garlic Rice with Halloumi	40
Pasta Shells Filled with Ricotta & Spinach	40
Creamy Chicken Pasta with Pesto Sauce	40

Chapter 6
Poultry — 41

Lebanese Grilled Chicken	42
Beans with Chicken Sausage and Escarole	42
Spinach and Chicken Pita Pizza	42
Herbed Roasted Chicken	43
Lemon and Paprika Herb-Marinated Chicken	44
Chicken with Potatoes	44
Braised Duck with Fennel Root	45
Chicken Shawarma	45
Lemon-Pepper Chicken Thighs	45
Chicken Fricassee with Red Cabbage	46
Marinated Chicken	46
Chicken Cacciatora	47
Skillet Creamy Tarragon Chicken and Mushrooms	47
Lemon-Garlic Chicken	48
Sheet Pan Pesto Chicken with Crispy Garlic Potatoes	48
Chicken and Potato Tagine	48

Chapter 7
Pork, Beef and Lamb — 49

Potato, Swiss Chard, and Lamb Hash	50
Beef Ragù	51

Beef Roast Braised with Onions	51	Vegetable Paella	71
Beef Tenderloin with Red Wine	52	Herbed Ricotta-Stuffed Mushrooms	71
Yogurt-and-Herb-Marinated Pork Tenderloin	52	Moroccan Vegetable Tagine	72
Pork & Mushroom Stew	53	Braised Carrots with Capers	72
Fennel Pork Estofado	53	Walnut Pesto Zoodles	73
Beef Brisket with Onions	53	Stuffed Cucumber Cups	73
Pressure Cooker Moroccan Pot Roast	54	Orange-Glazed Carrots	74
Pan-Roasted Lamb with Juniper Berries	54	Bite-Size Stuffed Peppers	74
Mediterranean Lamb Bowl	55	Lemon-Rosemary Beets	74
Herb-Roasted Beef Tips with Onions	55	Linguine and Brussels Sprouts	75
Shawarma Pork Tenderloin with Pitas	56	Spicy Roasted Potatoes	75
Beef and Goat Cheese Stuffed Peppers	57	Cauliflower Steaks with Eggplant Relish	76
Thin Lamb Chops Fried in Parmesan Batter	57	Fresh Veggie Frittata	76
Italian Tomato Glazes Pork Meatloaf	58	Smothered Cabbage	77
Lamb Burger	58	Citrus Asparagus with Pistachios	77
Egyptian Eggah with Ground Beef and Spinach	59		

Chapter 10
Desserts 78

Nut Butter Cup Fat Bomb	79
Homemade Sea Salt Pita Chips	79
Dark Chocolate Lava Cake	79
Baked Spanakopita Dip	80
Apple Chips with Chocolate Tahini	80
Pumpkin-Ricotta Cheesecake	81
Spiced Biscotti	81
Red Pepper Coques	82
Strawberry Caprese Skewers	83
Baked Apples with Amaretti Cookies	83
Lemon-Anise Biscotti	84
Chocolate Pudding	84
Manchego Crackers	85
Zesty Green Bites	85
Burrata Caprese Stack	86
Honey-Lavender Biscotti	86
Eggs with Spinach & Nuts	87
Olive Oil Ice Cream	87

Chapter 8
Fish and Seafood 60

Herbed Garlic Shrimp	61
Pan-Roasted Wild Cod with Tomatoes	61
Lemon Garlic Shrimp in Air Fryer	61
Shrimp with Tomatoes and Chili Pepper	62
Sea Bass with Roasted Root Vegetables	62
Steamed Cod with Garlic and Swiss Chard	63
Summer Mackerel Niçoise Platter	63
Juicy Air Fryer Salmon	64
Tomatoes Stuffed with Shrimp	65
Shrimp Ceviche Salad	65
Sweet and Sour Tuna Steaks	66
Parmesan Shrimp	66
Roasted Salmon with Fennel Salad	67
Roasted Branzino with Lemon	68
Salmon with Tarragon-Dijon Sauce	68
Air Fried Shrimp with Chili-Greek Yogurt Sauce	69

Appendix 1 Measurement Conversion Chart	88
Appendix 2 The Dirty Dozen and Clean Fifteen	89
Appendix 3 Index	90

Chapter 9
Vegetables and Vegan 70

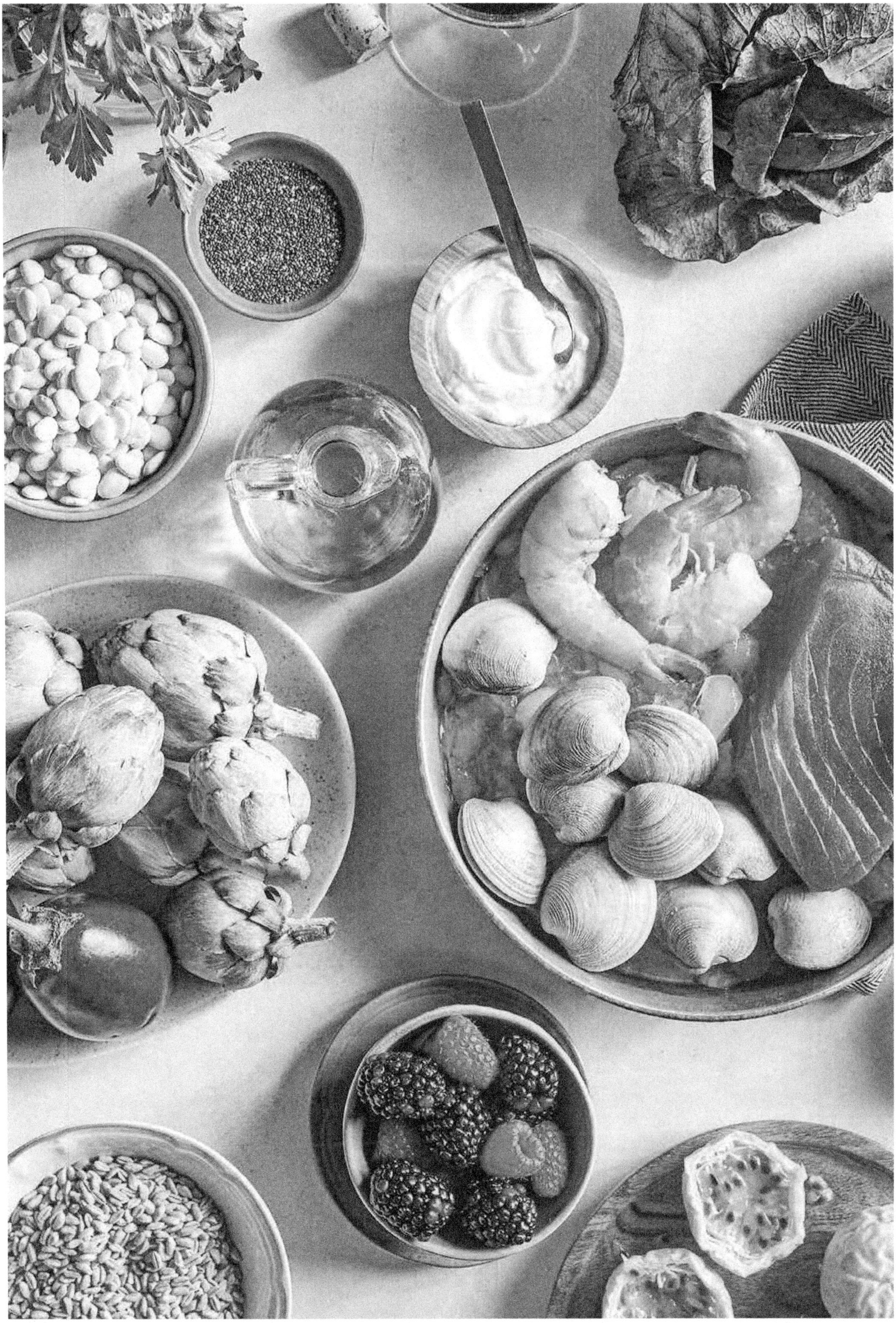

Introduction

Welcome to the vibrant and nourishing world of the Mediterranean diet! In these pages, you will embark on a culinary journey that celebrates not only the flavors of the Mediterranean but also the health benefits that have made this diet a global sensation.

The Mediterranean diet is not just a way of eating; it's a way of life. It hails from the picturesque regions surrounding the Mediterranean Sea, where the sun-drenched landscapes yield a bounty of fresh, colorful, and nutrient-rich ingredients. It's a diet rooted in tradition, with a history that stretches back thousands of years. But it's also a diet that's very much in tune with our modern understanding of nutrition and well-being.

As you flip through the pages of this cookbook, you'll discover a treasure trove of delicious recipes inspired by the Mediterranean diet. Whether you're a seasoned home cook or just starting on your culinary journey, you'll find something here to tantalize your taste buds and nourish your body.

The heart of the Mediterranean diet is its emphasis on whole, minimally processed foods. Fruits, vegetables, whole grains, legumes, and nuts take center stage in this diet, providing a rich source of vitamins, minerals, fiber, and antioxidants. These ingredients form the foundation of the recipes you'll find here, creating dishes that burst with flavor and nutritional goodness.

Olive oil, often referred to as "liquid gold," is another cornerstone of the Mediterranean diet. Its monounsaturated fats are believed to contribute to the diet's well-documented heart-protective properties. You'll see olive oil used liberally throughout these recipes, adding a luscious richness and depth of flavor to every dish.

Fish and seafood are also prominent in the Mediterranean diet. They provide lean protein and are a fantastic source of omega-3 fatty acids, which are known for their anti-inflammatory and heart-healthy benefits. From grilled sardines to baked salmon, you'll find a variety of seafood options that are as simple to prepare as they are delicious to savor.

Herbs and spices play a vital role in Mediterranean cuisine, elevating the taste of dishes without the need for excessive salt or unhealthy fats. The aromatic blend of basil, oregano, thyme, and more will transport you to the sun-soaked hills of Greece, Italy, and beyond.

One of the most appealing aspects of the Mediterranean diet is its adaptability. Whether you're a vegetarian, pescatarian, or prefer the occasional meat dish, you'll find recipes here that suit your dietary preferences. This diet is inclusive, embracing a wide range of food choices that cater to diverse tastes and lifestyles.

Beyond its delicious flavors, the Mediterranean diet is celebrated for its numerous health benefits. It has been linked to lower rates of heart disease, reduced risk of certain cancers, and improved cognitive function. It's also associated with weight management and a decreased risk of diabetes. But perhaps most importantly, it's a diet that promotes longevity and well-being, allowing you to savor life to the fullest.

In this cookbook, we invite you to embrace the Mediterranean diet not as a restrictive regimen but as a celebration of food, family, and health. Cook these recipes with love, share them with loved ones, and savor every bite. May these dishes become a part of your own culinary tradition, nourishing your body and soul for years to come.

So, let's embark on this Mediterranean culinary adventure together. Prepare to be delighted by the flavors, impressed by the health benefits, and inspired to make the Mediterranean diet a joyful and lifelong part of your own journey toward a healthier, happier you.

Buon appetito!

Chapter 1

Embracing a Mediterranean Lifestyle

Historical and Cultural Significance

The Mediterranean diet isn't just about what's on your plate; it's a profound reflection of history, culture, and the enduring human connection to the land and sea. As you embark on your culinary journey through these recipes, it's essential to grasp the deep roots and cultural tapestry that define the Mediterranean diet.

AN ANCIENT TRADITION

Imagine ancient Greek philosophers gathered around a table laden with olives, figs, and wine, engaging in profound discussions about life's mysteries. This scene, though millennia old, embodies the essence of the Mediterranean diet. It was a way of life for ancient civilizations, from the Greeks and Romans to the Egyptians and Phoenicians.

The diet's roots extend back to the simple agrarian practices of these early societies. The cultivation of olive trees, the planting of vineyards, and the harvesting of grains were not just means of sustenance; they were rituals that bound communities together and connected people to their ancestral lands.

CULTURAL CONNECTION TO THE LAND AND SEA

One of the most remarkable aspects of the Mediterranean diet is its deep connection to the region's geography. The diet is a reflection of the Mediterranean's diverse landscapes, from the sun-drenched coastlines to the fertile valleys and rugged mountains.

Coastal communities embraced the riches of the sea, incorporating fish and seafood into their daily fare. Inland villages thrived on the bounty of their orchards and fields, producing a vibrant array of fruits, vegetables, and grains. This regional diversity led to an incredible variety of flavors and culinary traditions, each shaped by the land's offerings.

TRADITIONS PASSED DOWN THROUGH GENERATIONS

The Mediterranean diet is more than just a list of ingredients; it's a repository of knowledge, passed down through generations. Families gather to prepare and share traditional dishes, often following recipes that have remained unchanged for centuries.

Grandmothers teach their grandchildren the art of making pasta by hand, preserving the secrets of generations in each knead and fold. Parents pass on the importance of harvesting olives and pressing them into liquid gold. In these traditions, the Mediterranean diet lives on as a tangible link to the past.

A MODERN CONNECTION TO TIMELESS VALUES

In today's fast-paced world, the Mediterranean diet stands as a symbol of timeless values. It champions the art of slow dining, emphasizing leisurely meals shared with family and friends. It encourages mindful eating, savoring each bite and appreciating the flavors of fresh, seasonal ingredients.

As you explore the recipes in this cookbook, consider the cultural depth that each dish carries. Each recipe is a snapshot of history, a taste of the past that you can bring to your modern table. In every bite of Mediterranean cuisine, you connect with a tradition that has nourished body and soul for centuries.

Benefits of the Mediterranean Diet

The Mediterranean Diet, renowned for its remarkable health advantages, is more than just a meal plan; it's a lifestyle that embodies the essence of well-being. Rooted in the dietary patterns of Mediterranean countries like Greece, Italy, and Spain, this diet has been celebrated for centuries. Today, it continues to captivate researchers and health enthusiasts alike. In this comprehensive overview, we'll delve into the myriad benefits of the Mediterranean Diet, exploring its impact on heart health, longevity, weight management, cognitive function, and more.

HEART HEALTH

One of the most widely recognized benefits of the Mediterranean Diet is its profound impact on heart health. Research consistently shows that individuals who adhere to this diet are at a significantly lower risk of heart disease. Here's why:

- Healthy Fats: The Mediterranean Diet places a heavy emphasis on monounsaturated fats found in olive oil and nuts. These fats have been associated with reduced levels of "bad" LDL cholesterol and decreased risk of atherosclerosis (hardening of the arteries).
- Omega-3 Fatty Acids: Regular consumption of fatty fish, such as salmon and sardines, provides a rich source of omega-3 fatty acids. These essential fats help lower blood pressure and reduce inflammation, crucial factors in heart disease prevention.
- Antioxidants: Fruits and vegetables rich in antioxidants, like tomatoes and berries, protect blood vessels from damage and improve overall cardiovascular health.
- Moderate Alcohol: Some Mediterranean cultures incorporate moderate red wine consumption, which has been linked to a reduced risk of heart disease, thanks to compounds like resveratrol.

LONGEVITY

The Mediterranean Diet is often associated with increased longevity. Populations in Mediterranean regions have a higher proportion of centenarians – individuals who live to be over 100 years old. The diet's role in promoting longevity can be attributed to several factors:

- Nutrient Density: A diet abundant in fruits, vegetables, whole grains, and lean proteins provides a wealth of essential nutrients and antioxidants that support overall health.
- Healthy Fats: Monounsaturated fats in olive oil, nuts, and seeds may contribute to a longer, healthier life by reducing the risk of chronic diseases.
- Moderate Portions: The Mediterranean Diet encourages mindful eating and modest portion sizes, which may prevent overeating and promote a healthy weight.
- Social Engagement: The Mediterranean lifestyle emphasizes the importance of social connections, leisurely meals, and a sense of community, factors that contribute to overall well-being and longevity.

WEIGHT MANAGEMENT

In an era when obesity rates are soaring, the Mediterranean Diet stands out as a

practical and effective approach to weight management:
- Satiety: Meals rich in fiber, protein, and healthy fats keep you feeling fuller for longer, reducing the likelihood of overeating and snacking between meals.
- Balanced Nutrients: The diet provides a wide range of nutrients without excessive calories, making it easier to maintain a healthy weight.
- Sustainable: Unlike many fad diets, the Mediterranean Diet is sustainable in the long term, helping individuals maintain their weight loss and overall health.
- Physical Activity: The Mediterranean lifestyle encourages regular physical activity, another key component of maintaining a healthy weight.

COGNITIVE FUNCTION

Emerging research suggests that the Mediterranean Diet may have a protective effect on cognitive function, reducing the risk of cognitive decline and neurodegenerative diseases such as Alzheimer's:
- Brain-Boosting Nutrients: Antioxidants, vitamins, and minerals from fruits and vegetables help protect brain cells from oxidative damage.
- Omega-3 Fatty Acids: The diet's emphasis on fatty fish provides essential omega-3s, which are associated with improved cognitive function and memory.
- Blood Flow: Olive oil's role in promoting healthy blood flow to the brain may contribute to cognitive health.
- Inflammation Reduction: The diet's anti-inflammatory properties may protect against brain inflammation, a contributing factor in cognitive decline.

DIABETES PREVENTION AND MANAGEMENT

The Mediterranean Diet can be a valuable tool in preventing and managing diabetes:
- Blood Sugar Control: The diet's emphasis on whole grains, legumes, and fiber-rich foods helps regulate blood sugar levels, reducing the risk of type 2 diabetes.
- Weight Management: By promoting a healthy weight, the Mediterranean Diet decreases the risk of developing diabetes.
- Heart Health: The diet's heart-healthy components also benefit individuals with diabetes, as cardiovascular health is closely linked to diabetes management.
- Healthy Fats: Monounsaturated fats help improve insulin sensitivity, a critical factor in diabetes control.

CANCER RISK REDUCTION

Research suggests that the Mediterranean Diet may have a protective effect against certain types of cancer:
- Antioxidants: The diet's abundance of fruits and vegetables provides a rich source of antioxidants, which help neutralize harmful free radicals linked to cancer development.
- Omega-3s: The presence of omega-3 fatty acids in fatty fish is associated with a reduced risk of several cancers, including breast and colorectal cancer.
- Fiber: High-fiber foods in the diet, like whole grains and legumes, are believed to lower the risk of digestive tract cancers.
- Phytonutrients: Plant-based compounds in the Mediterranean Diet, such as flavonoids and polyphenols, have shown promise in preventing cancer.

BETTER DIGESTIVE HEALTH

The Mediterranean Diet's emphasis on whole grains, fiber-rich foods, and fermented dairy products can promote optimal digestive health:
- Fiber: High-fiber foods support regular bowel movements and prevent constipation.
- Gut Microbiome: The diet's inclusion of yogurt and other fermented foods contributes to a healthy gut microbiome, which is essential for digestion and overall well-being.
- Digestive Disorders: Some research suggests that the diet's anti-inflammatory properties may benefit individuals with digestive disorders like irritable bowel syndrome (IBS).

ANTI-INFLAMMATORY PROPERTIES

Chronic inflammation is a contributing factor to various chronic diseases, from heart disease to arthritis. The Mediterranean Diet's anti-inflammatory components include:
- Olive Oil: Rich in monounsaturated fats and anti-inflammatory compounds, olive oil has been shown to reduce inflammatory markers in the body.
- Fruits and Vegetables: The diet's abundance of colorful produce contains natural anti-inflammatory agents like polyphenols and flavonoids.
- Fatty Fish: Omega-3 fatty acids in fish like salmon and mackerel have anti-inflammatory properties.
- Herbs and Spices: The Mediterranean Diet's use of herbs and spices, such as turmeric and garlic, adds flavor while providing potential anti-inflammatory benefits.

LOWER RISK OF METABOLIC SYNDROME

Metabolic syndrome is a cluster of conditions that increase the risk of heart disease, stroke, and type 2 diabetes. The Mediterranean Diet's components can help reduce the risk factors associated with metabolic syndrome:
- Weight Management: The diet supports healthy weight maintenance and reduces abdominal obesity, a key factor in metabolic syndrome.
- Blood Pressure: The diet's emphasis on fruits, vegetables, and healthy fats can help lower blood pressure, a component of metabolic syndrome.
- Blood Sugar: By regulating blood sugar levels, the diet reduces the risk of metabolic syndrome and type 2 diabetes.
- Lipid Profile: The diet's influence on cholesterol levels helps improve the lipid profile, another factor in metabolic syndrome.

OVERALL WELL-BEING

Finally, the Mediterranean Diet isn't just about physical health; it's also about mental and emotional well-being:
- Improved Mood: The consumption of nutrient-rich foods may enhance mood and reduce the risk of depression and anxiety.
- Social Engagement: The Mediterranean lifestyle emphasizes communal dining, fostering a sense of belonging and emotional support.
- Leisurely Eating: Slow, mindful meals encourage relaxation and enjoyment of food, reducing stress and promoting well-being.
- Quality of Life: By reducing the risk of chronic diseases and promoting overall health, the Mediterranean Diet enhances the quality of life for those who follow it.

Stocking Your Mediterranean Pantry

Creating authentic Mediterranean dishes begins with a well-stocked pantry filled with essential ingredients that form the foundation of this renowned cuisine.

OLIVE OIL: THE LIQUID GOLD

At the heart of Mediterranean cooking lies olive oil, often referred to as "liquid gold." It's not only a staple but also a symbol of the Mediterranean diet's health benefits. Opt for extra-virgin olive oil, which retains the most nutrients and robust flavor. Use it for sautéing, drizzling over salads, and as a flavorful finishing touch to dishes.

FRESH HERBS AND SPICES: AROMATIC MAGIC

The Mediterranean pantry is brimming with herbs and spices that infuse dishes with vibrant flavors. Essentials include basil, oregano, thyme, rosemary, parsley, and mint. Additionally, spices like cumin, coriander, cinnamon, and paprika add depth and complexity to Mediterranean dishes. Use these seasonings generously but mindfully to enhance your culinary creations.

WHOLE GRAINS: THE BASIS OF SUSTENANCE

Whole grains are a cornerstone of Mediterranean cuisine, providing a source of sustained energy and fiber. Stock your pantry with staples like whole wheat couscous, bulgur, farro, and brown rice. These grains serve as the perfect canvas for Mediterranean-inspired dishes, from grain salads to pilafs.

FRUITS AND VEGETABLES: FRESH AND FLAVORFUL

A bounty of fruits and vegetables is essential for Mediterranean cooking. Opt for fresh, seasonal produce whenever possible. Tomatoes, bell peppers, cucumbers, eggplants, zucchini, and leafy greens are common Mediterranean ingredients. Canned tomatoes, sun-dried tomatoes, and roasted red peppers can also be handy for off-season dishes.

NUTS AND SEEDS: CRUNCHY GOODNESS

Nuts and seeds not only add texture but also a wealth of nutrients to your Mediterranean creations. Almonds, walnuts, pistachios, and pine nuts are commonly used. Sesame seeds, both raw and toasted, provide a delightful nutty flavor and are an essential ingredient in tahini.

LEGUMES: PLANT-BASED PROTEIN

Legumes like chickpeas, lentils, and beans are a rich source of plant-based protein and fiber. Stock your pantry with both dried and canned options for convenience. Use them in soups, stews, salads, and spreads like hummus.

FISH AND SEAFOOD: FROM THE OCEAN'S BOUNTY

Mediterranean cuisine celebrates the ocean's gifts. Keep a supply of canned or jarred tuna, sardines, and anchovies for quick and convenient protein sources. Fresh or frozen seafood like salmon, mackerel, and shrimp are versatile ingredients for grilling, baking, or pan-searing.

DAIRY AND DAIRY ALTERNATIVES: CREAMY AND NUTRITIOUS

Greek yogurt is a Mediterranean pantry staple, serving as a protein-rich base for both sweet and savory dishes. Feta cheese, goat cheese, and Parmesan are also commonly used. If you're opting for dairy alternatives, stock almond milk, soy yogurt, or other plant-based options.

PASTA AND BREAD: COMFORTING CARBS

Pasta, particularly whole wheat or semolina varieties, is a versatile Mediterranean ingredient. Choose shapes like penne, spaghetti, or orzo to complement your recipes. Additionally, keep pita bread or whole-grain bread for sandwiches and dipping into olive oil and spices.

CONDIMENTS AND VINEGARS: FLAVOR ENHANCERS

Condiments like tahini, harissa, and pomegranate molasses are flavor powerhouses that elevate Mediterranean dishes. Vinegars such as red wine vinegar and balsamic vinegar add acidity and depth to dressings and marinades. Don't forget to stock honey for a touch of natural sweetness.

CANNED GOODS: CONVENIENCE WITHOUT COMPROMISE

Canned goods like artichoke hearts, olives, and capers are convenient additions to Mediterranean recipes. They add briny, tangy, and savory elements that enhance the complexity of your dishes. Ensure you have a variety of olives on hand, from Kalamata to green to black.

WINE AND SPIRITS: A TOAST TO TRADITION

While not a pantry staple, wine, especially red wine, is integral to Mediterranean dining traditions. A glass of red wine complements many dishes and is often enjoyed in moderation. Consider stocking a bottle of your favorite Mediterranean varietal to complete your culinary experience.

Chapter 2

28-Day Meal Plan

Week 1: Embracing the Mediterranean Diet

Congratulations on taking the first step towards a healthier lifestyle with the Mediterranean Diet! This week marks the beginning of a transformative journey that will reward you with improved well-being and vitality. Embrace the simplicity and richness of this diet, focusing on nourishing your body with wholesome, nutrient-packed foods. As you make mindful choices, remember that every small change you make is a step closer to a healthier you. Stay committed and motivated, and soon you'll begin to experience the positive impact of this new way of eating.

Meal Plan	Breakfast	Lunch	Dinner	Snack
Day-1	Carrot Bread	Chicken Cacciatora	Orange-Glazed Carrots	Red Pepper Coques
Day-2	Carrot Bread	Chicken Cacciatora	Orange-Glazed Carrots	Red Pepper Coques
Day-3	Carrot Bread	Chicken Cacciatora	Orange-Glazed Carrots	Red Pepper Coques
Day-4	Carrot Bread	Chicken Cacciatora	Orange-Glazed Carrots	Red Pepper Coques
Day-5	Carrot Bread	Chicken Cacciatora	Orange-Glazed Carrots	Red Pepper Coques

Shopping List for Week 1

PROTEINS:
- 3- to 4-pound chicken, cut into 6 to 8 pieces
- 2 eggs

VEGETABLES:
- 1½ cups carrots, peeled and grated
- 3 pounds carrots, peeled and cut into ¼-inch slices on the bias
- 2 large onions, halved and sliced thin
- 2 cups jarred roasted red peppers, patted dry and sliced thin
- 3 garlic cloves, peeled and sliced very thin
- 3 to 4 cups fresh, very ripe, firm meaty tomatoes, skinned raw with a peeler and chopped, or canned imported Italian plum tomatoes, cut up, with their juice

MISCELLANEOUS:
- 1 cup all-purpose flour
- 1 teaspoon baking soda
- ½ teaspoon ground cinnamon
- ¼ teaspoon ground cloves
- ¼ teaspoon ground nutmeg
- ½ teaspoon salt
- ¾ cup vegetable oil
- 1/3 cup white sugar
- 1/3 cup light brown sugar
- ½ cup extra-virgin olive oil
- ¼ teaspoon red pepper flakes
- 2 bay leaves
- 3 tablespoons sherry vinegar
- ¼ cup pine nuts (optional)
- 1 tablespoon minced fresh parsley

Week 2: Diving Deeper into Mediterranean Delights

As you enter Week 2, you're delving deeper into the Mediterranean way of life. Embrace the joy of discovering new flavors and aromas that will awaken your taste buds and inspire your culinary adventures. Your commitment to choosing fresh, natural ingredients is already paying off, and you'll soon notice positive changes in your energy levels and overall well-being. Stay focused on the journey, and remember that each day brings you closer to unlocking the full potential of this nourishing diet.

Meal Plan	Breakfast	Lunch	Dinner	Snack
Day-1	Thin-Crust Pizza	Beef Brisket with Onions	Beef Brisket with Onions	Zesty Green Bites
Day-2	Thin-Crust Pizza	Beef Brisket with Onions	Parmesan Shrimp	Zesty Green Bites
Day-3	Thin-Crust Pizza	Beef Brisket with Onions	Parmesan Shrimp	Zesty Green Bites
Day-4	Thin-Crust Pizza	Beef Brisket with Onions	Parmesan Shrimp	Zesty Green Bites
Day-5	Thin-Crust Pizza	Beef Brisket with Onions	Parmesan Shrimp	Zesty Green Bites

Shopping List for Week 2

PROTEINS:
- 1 first cut of beef brisket (4 pounds), trimmed of excess fat
- 8 cups peeled, deveined jumbo cooked shrimp

VEGETABLES:
- 1 large yellow onion, thinly sliced
- 2 large garlic cloves (for slicing and mincing)
- ¼ cup frozen chopped kale
- ¼ cup finely chopped artichoke hearts

FRUITS:
- 1 large lemon (for zest and wedges)

MISCELLANEOUS:

- 3 cups (16½ ounces) bread flour
- 2 teaspoons sugar
- ½ teaspoon instant or rapid-rise yeast
- 1⅓ cups ice water
- 1 tablespoon extra-virgin olive oil
- 1½ teaspoons salt
- 1 (28-ounce) can whole peeled tomatoes, drained with juice reserved
- 1 tablespoon extra-virgin olive oil
- 1 teaspoon red wine vinegar
- 1 teaspoon dried oregano
- ½ teaspoon salt
- ¼ teaspoon pepper
- 4 cloves of minced garlic
- ½ teaspoon oregano
- 1 teaspoon basil
- ¼ cup goat cheese
- 1 large egg white
- 1 tsp dried basil
- 1 tbsp extra-virgin olive oil

Week 3: Unleashing the Mediterranean Secrets

Week 3 brings a sense of empowerment as you uncover the secrets of the Mediterranean Diet's numerous health benefits. By now, you've experienced firsthand how this way of eating can transform your body and mind. As you continue to fuel your body with wholesome foods, embrace the sense of clarity and vitality that comes with it. Celebrate your progress and remember that you have the strength and determination to carry this newfound lifestyle beyond the four weeks. Let the Mediterranean Diet become a part of who you are and bring out the best version of yourself.

Meal Plan	Breakfast	Lunch	Dinner	Snack
Day-1	Dilled Tuna Salad Sandwich	Sweet and Sour Tuna Steaks	Moroccan Vegetable Tagine	Olive Oil Ice Cream
Day-2	Dilled Tuna Salad Sandwich	Sweet and Sour Tuna Steaks	Moroccan Vegetable Tagine	Olive Oil Ice Cream
Day-3	Dilled Tuna Salad Sandwich	Sweet and Sour Tuna Steaks	Moroccan Vegetable Tagine	Olive Oil Ice Cream
Day-4	Caprese Scrambled Eggs	Sweet and Sour Tuna Steaks	Moroccan Vegetable Tagine	Olive Oil Ice Cream
Day-5	Caprese Scrambled Eggs	Sweet and Sour Tuna Steaks	Moroccan Vegetable Tagine	Olive Oil Ice Cream

Shopping List for Week 3

PROTEINS:
- 2 (4-ounce) cans tuna, packed in olive oil
- 4 eggs
- 2½ pounds fresh tuna, cut into ½-inch-thick steaks
- 4 large egg yolks

VEGETABLES:
- 1 very ripe avocado, peeled, pitted, and mashed
- 1 tablespoon chopped fresh capers (optional)
- 1 cup button mushrooms, chopped
- 1 large tomato, chopped
- 2 spring onions, chopped
- 2 medium yellow onions, sliced
- 6 celery stalks, sliced into ¼-inch crescents
- 6 garlic cloves, minced
- 2 cups cauliflower florets
- 1 (13.75-ounce) can artichoke hearts, drained and quartered

MISCELLANEOUS:
- 4 Versatile Sandwich Rounds (bread or buns)
- ½ cup fresh mozzarella cheese
- ¼ cup milk
- 2 tbsp olive oil
- ½ tsp salt
- 3 cups onion, sliced very, very thin
- black pepper, ground fresh from the mill
- 2 tablespoons chopped parsley
- ½ teaspoon paprika
- ½ teaspoon ground cinnamon
- ¼ teaspoon freshly ground black pepper
- 2 cups vegetable stock
- 1 cup halved and pitted green olives

Week 4: Celebrating Your Transformative Journey

Congratulations! You've made it to Week 4, and you're now fully immersed in the Mediterranean lifestyle. Your commitment to wholesome, unprocessed foods has yielded tremendous rewards, both physically and mentally. Embrace this final week with gratitude and a sense of accomplishment. Continue enjoying a rainbow of fresh produce, indulge in occasional glasses of red wine, and prioritize regular physical activity. By now, you'll likely notice improved digestion, glowing skin, and a balanced weight. As you conclude this transformative journey, remember that the Mediterranean Diet isn't just a month-long endeavor; it's a lifelong celebration of health and well-being. Embrace this lifestyle with joy, and may it bring you lasting vitality and happiness.

Meal Plan	Breakfast	Lunch	Dinner	Snack
Day-1	Broccoli and Feta Frittata	Beef Ragù	Smothered Cabbage	Pumpkin-Ricotta Cheesecake
Day-2	Broccoli and Feta Frittata	Beef Ragù	Smothered Cabbage	Pumpkin-Ricotta Cheesecake
Day-3	Broccoli and Feta Frittata	Beef Ragù	Smothered Cabbage	Pumpkin-Ricotta Cheesecake
Day-4	Broccoli and Feta Frittata	Beef Ragù	Smothered Cabbage	Pumpkin-Ricotta Cheesecake
Day-5	Broccoli and Feta Frittata	Beef Ragù	Smothered Cabbage	Pumpkin-Ricotta Cheesecake

Shopping List for Week 4

PROTEINS:
- 16 large eggs
- One 4-pound beef chuck roast, halved

VEGETABLES:
- 12 ounces broccoli florets, cut into ½-inch pieces (3½ to 4 cups)
- 2 medium yellow onion, diced small
- 2 pounds green, red, or savoy cabbage

MISCELLANEOUS:
- ⅓ cup whole milk
- 1 tablespoon extra-virgin olive oil
- Pinch red pepper flakes
- ½ teaspoon grated lemon zest plus ½ teaspoon juice
- 4 ounces feta cheese, crumbled into ½-inch pieces (1 cup)
- 3 cloves garlic, minced
- 6 tablespoons tomato paste
- 3 tablespoons chopped fresh oregano leaves (or 3 teaspoons dried oregano)
- Coarse sea salt
- Black pepper
- 2 cups beef stock
- 2 tablespoons red wine vinegar
- ½ cup extra virgin olive oil
- 1 (14.5-ounce) can pumpkin purée
- 8 ounces cream cheese, at room temperature
- ½ cup whole-milk ricotta cheese
- ½ to ¾ cup sugar-free sweetener
- 2 teaspoons vanilla extract
- 2 teaspoons pumpkin pie spice

Chapter 3

Breakfast and Brunch

Ratatouille with Poached Eggs

Prep time: 5 minutes | Cook time 25 minutes | Serves 4

- ¼ cup extra-virgin olive oil
- 1 pound zucchini, cut into ¾-inch pieces
- 1 pound eggplant, cut into ¾-inch pieces
- Salt and pepper
- 1 onion, chopped fine
- 4 garlic cloves, minced
- 1 pound plum tomatoes, cored and cut into ½-inch pieces
- ½ cup chicken or vegetable broth
- 4 large eggs
- ¼ cup chopped fresh basil
- 1 ounce Parmesan cheese, grated (½ cup)

1. Heat 1 tablespoon oil in 12-inch nonstick skillet over medium-high heat until just smoking. Add zucchini and cook until well browned, about 5 minutes; transfer to bowl.
2. Add eggplant, 2 tablespoons oil, and ¼ teaspoon salt to now-empty skillet and cook over medium-high heat until eggplant is browned, 5 to 7 minutes. Stir in onion and remaining 1 tablespoon oil and cook until onion is softened, about 5 minutes. Stir in garlic and cook until fragrant, about 30 seconds. Stir in tomatoes and broth and simmer until vegetables are softened, 3 to 5 minutes. Stir in zucchini and any accumulated juice and season with salt and pepper to taste.
3. Off heat, make 4 shallow indentations (about 2 inches wide) in surface of ratatouille using back of spoon. Crack 1 egg into each indentation and season with salt and pepper. Cover and cook over medium-low heat until egg whites are just set and yolks are still runny, 4 to 6 minutes. Sprinkle with basil and Parmesan and serve immediately.

Israeli Eggplant and Egg Sandwiches

Prep time: 5 minutes | Cook time 15 minutes | Serves 4

- 1 pound eggplant, sliced into ½-inch-thick rounds
- Salt and pepper
- ¼ cup extra-virgin olive oil
- 8 ounces cherry tomatoes, quartered
- ½ cup finely chopped dill pickles
- ¼ cup finely chopped red onion
- ¼ cup fresh parsley leaves
- 1 tablespoon lemon juice
- 1 garlic clove, minced
- 4 (8-inch) pita breads
- 1 cup hummus
- 6 hard-cooked large eggs, sliced thin
- ½ cup Tahini-Yogurt Sauce
- ½ cup Green Zhoug
- 1 teaspoon ground dried Aleppo pepper

1. Spread eggplant on baking sheet lined with paper towels, sprinkle both sides with 2 teaspoons salt, and let sit for 30 minutes.
2. Adjust oven rack 4 inches from broiler element and heat broiler. Thoroughly pat eggplant dry with paper towels, arrange on aluminum foil–lined rimmed Broil eggplant until spotty brown, about 5 minutes per side.
3. Combine tomatoes, pickles, onion, parsley, lemon juice, garlic, and remaining 2 tablespoons oil in bowl and season with salt and pepper to taste. Lay each pita on individual plate, spread with ¼ cup hummus, and top evenly with eggplant, tomato salad, and eggs. Drizzle with Tahini-Yogurt Sauce and Green Zhoug and sprinkle with Aleppo. Serve immediately.

Garlic & Bell Pepper Frittata

Prep time: 5 minutes | Cook time: 20 minutes | Serves 2

- 2 red bell peppers, chopped
- 4 eggs
- 2 tbsp olive oil
- 2 garlic cloves, crushed
- 1 tsp Italian Seasoning mix

1. Grease the pot with oil. Stir-fry the peppers for 2-3 minutes, or until lightly charred. Set aside. Add garlic and stir-fry for 1 minute, until soft.
2. Whisk the eggs and season with Italian seasoning. Pour the mixture into the pot and cook for 2-3 minutes, or until set. Using a spatula, loosen the edges and gently slide onto a plate. Add charred peppers and fold over. Serve hot.

Caprese Scrambled Eggs

Prep time: 5 minutes | Cook time: 25 minutes | Serves 2

- 4 eggs
- ½ cup fresh mozzarella cheese
- 1 cup button mushrooms, chopped
- 1 large tomato, chopped
- 2 spring onions, chopped
- ¼ cup milk
- 2 tbsp olive oil
- ½ tsp salt

1. Grease the pot with oil and set on Sauté. Stir-fry the onions for 3 minutes, or until translucent. Add tomatoes and mushrooms.
2. Cook until liquid evaporates, for 5-6 minutes. Meanwhile, Whisk eggs, cheese, milk, and salt. Pour into the pot and stir. Cook for 2 minutes, or until set.

Carrot Bread

Prep time: 15 minutes | Cook time: 30 minutes | Serves 6

- 1 cup of all-purpose flour
- 1 teaspoon baking soda
- ½ teaspoon ground cinnamon
- ¼ teaspoon ground nutmeg
- ½ teaspoon salt
- 2 eggs
- ¾ cup vegetable oil
- 1/3 cup white sugar
- 1/3 cup light brown sugar
- ½ teaspoon vanilla extract
- 1½ cups carrots, peeled and grated

1. In a bowl, mix the baking soda, flour, spices, and salt.
2. Add the eggs, sugars, oil, and vanilla extract to another bowl and beat until well combined. Add the flour mixture and mix. Fold in the carrots. Place the mixture into a greased baking pan.
3. Press the "Power Button" of the Air Fryer and select the "Air Fry." Set the cooking time to thirty minutes | and the temperature at 320° F. Press Start.
4. When the unit beeps, open the lid.
5. Arrange the pan in the Air Fryer Basket and insert it into the oven. Place the pan onto a wire rack to cool for about ten minutes.
6. Cut the bread into desired-sized slices and serve.

16 | The Mediterranean Diet Cookbook for Beginners

Italian Ricotta & Tomato Omelet

Prep time: 5 minutes | Cook time: 30 minutes | Serves 4

- 1 lb tomatoes, peeled, roughly diced
- 1 tbsp tomato paste
- 1 tsp brown sugar
- 1 cup ricotta cheese
- 4 eggs
- 3 tbsp olive oil
- 1 tbsp Italian seasoning mix
- ¼ cup fresh parsley, chopped
- ¼ tsp salt

1. Grease the inner pot with oil. Press Sauté and add tomatoes, sugar, Italian seasoning, parsley, and salt. Give it a good stir and cook for 15 minutes or until the tomatoes soften. Stir occasionally.
2. Meanwhile, whisk eggs and cheese. Pour the mixture into the pot stir well. Cook for 3 more minutes. Serve immediately.

Scrambled Eggs with Feta and Olives

Prep time: 5 minutes | Cook time: 15 minutes | Serves 2

- 4 large eggs
- 1 tablespoon milk
- Sea salt, to taste
- 1 tablespoon olive oil
- 1/4 cup crumbled feta cheese
- 10 Kalamata olives, pitted and sliced
- Freshly ground pepper, to taste
- Small bunch fresh mint, chopped, for garnish

1. Beat the eggs with a fork or wire whisk until just combined. Add the milk and a pinch of sea salt.
2. Heat a medium nonstick skillet over medium-high heat and add the olive oil.
3. Add the eggs and stir constantly, until they just begin to curd and firm up. Add the feta cheese and olives, and stir until evenly combined.
4. Season with sea salt and freshly ground pepper to taste. Use a light hand with the salt, because the olives and feta are very salty.
5. Divide between 2 plates and garnish with the fresh chopped mint. Serve immediately.

Cauliflower Pizza Crusts

Prep time: 10 minutes | Cook time: 30 minutes | Serves 2

- One cup cauliflower rice
- 1/2 tbsp. Tapioca starch
- 1/2 cup vegan grated mozzarella
- 1/8 tsp. salt
- One clove garlic, peeled and minced
- 1 tsp. Italian seasoning

1. Preheat and set the Air Fryer's temperature to 400 degrees F for three minutes.
2. In a medium bowl, combine all ingredients.
3. Divide the mixture in half and spread it into two pizza pans lightly greased with oil.
4. Place one pan in the Air Fryer basket and cook for twelve minutes. Once done, remove the pan from the basket and repeat with the second pan.
5. Top crusts with your favorite toppings and cook an additional three minutes.

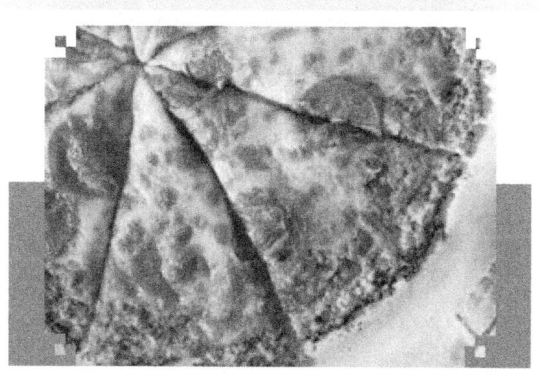

Cranberry Bread

Prep time: 15 minutes | Cook time: 30 minutes | Serves 10

- Four eggs
- Three cups flour
- 2/3 cups sugar
- 2/3 cup vegetable oil
- ½ cup milk
- 1 teaspoon vanilla extract
- 2 teaspoons baking powder
- 2 cups fresh cranberries

1. In a bowl, add all the ingredients (except the cranberries) and stir until well combined.
2. Gently fold in the cranberries.
3. Place the mixture into a lightly greased baking pan evenly. Select the "Air Fry" mode. Press the Time button and set the cooking time to thirty mins. Then push the Temp button and rotate the dial to set the temperature at 320° F.
4. Press the Start button. When the unit beeps, open the lid.
5. Arrange the pan in the basket of the Air Fryer and insert it in the oven. Place the pan onto a wire rack and cook for about 10-15 mins.
6. Carefully invert the bread onto the wire rack to cool completely before slicing. Cut the bread into desired-sized slices.

Dilled Tuna Salad Sandwich

Prep time: 10 minutes | Cook time: 5 minutes | Serves 4

- 4 Versatile Sandwich Rounds
- 2 (4-ounce) cans tuna, packed in olive oil
- 2 tablespoons Roasted Garlic Aioli, or avocado oil mayonnaise with 1 to 2 teaspoons freshly squeezed lemon juice and/or zest
- 1 very ripe avocado, peeled, pitted, and mashed
- 1 tablespoon chopped fresh capers (optional)
- 1 teaspoon chopped fresh dill or ½ teaspoon dried dill

1. Make sandwich rounds according to recipe. Cut each round in half and set aside.
2. In a medium bowl, place the tuna and the oil from cans. Add the aioli, avocado, capers (if using), and dill and blend well with a fork.
3. Toast sandwich rounds and fill each with one-quarter of the tuna salad, about ⅓ cup.

Peachy Green Smoothie

Prep time: 5 minutes | Cook time: 15 minutes | Serves 2

- 1 cup almond milk
- 3 cups kale or spinach
- 1 banana, peeled
- 1 orange, peeled
- 1 small green apple
- 1 cup frozen peaches
- 1/4 cup vanilla Greek yogurt

1. Put the ingredients in a blender in the order listed and blend on high until smooth.
2. Serve and enjoy.

Fried Eggs with Potato and Parmesan Pancake

Prep time: 5 minutes | Cook time 35 minutes | Serves 8

- 2½ pounds Yukon Gold potatoes, peeled and shredded
- 1½ teaspoons cornstarch
- Salt and pepper
- ¼ cup plus 2 teaspoons extra-virgin olive oil
- 8 large eggs
- 1 ounce Parmesan cheese, grated (½ cup)
- 1 tablespoon minced fresh chives

1. Place potatoes in large bowl and fill bowl with cold water. Using hands, swirl to remove excess starch, then drain, leaving potatoes in colander.
2. Wipe bowl dry. Place one-third of potatoes in center of clean dish towel. Gather towel ends together and twist tightly to squeeze out moisture. Transfer potatoes to now-empty bowl and repeat process with remaining potatoes in 2 batches.
3. Sprinkle cornstarch, 1 teaspoon salt, and pinch pepper over potatoes. Using hands or fork, toss ingredients together until well combined.
4. Heat 2 tablespoons oil in 12-inch nonstick skillet over medium heat until shimmering. Add potato mixture and spread into even layer. Cover and cook for 6 minutes. Uncover and, using spatula, gently press potatoes down to form round cake. Cook, occasionally pressing on potatoes to shape into uniform round cake, until bottom is deep golden brown, 8 to 10 minutes.
5. Shake skillet to loosen pancake and slide onto large plate. Add 2 tablespoons oil to skillet and swirl to coat. Invert potato pancake onto second plate and slide potato pancake, browned side up, back into skillet. Cook, occasionally pressing down on pancake, until bottom is well browned, 8 to 10 minutes. Transfer pancake to cutting board and set aside while preparing eggs.
6. Crack eggs into 2 small bowls (4 eggs per bowl) and season with salt and pepper. Wipe skillet clean with paper towels. Heat remaining 2 teaspoons oil in now-empty skillet over medium heat until shimmering. Working quickly, pour 1 bowl of eggs in 1 side of skillet and second bowl of eggs in other side. Cover and cook for 2 minutes.
7. Remove skillet from heat and let sit, covered, about 2 minutes for runny yolks (white around edge of yolk will be barely opaque), about 3 minutes for soft but set yolks, and about 4 minutes for medium-set yolks. Slide eggs onto individual plates. Sprinkle pancake with Parmesan and chives, cut into wedges, and serve with eggs.

The Mediterranean Diet Cookbook for Beginners

Spanish Tortilla with Roasted Red Peppers

Prep time: 5 minutes | Cook time 30 minutes | Serves 6

- 1½ pounds Yukon Gold potatoes, peeled, quartered, and sliced ⅛ inch thick
- 1 small onion, halved and sliced thin
- 6 tablespoons plus 1 teaspoon extra-virgin olive oil
- Salt and pepper
- 8 large eggs
- ½ cup jarred roasted red peppers, rinsed, patted dry, and cut into ½-inch pieces
- ½ cup frozen peas, thawed

1. Toss potatoes and onion with ¼ cup oil, ½ teaspoon salt, and ¼ teaspoon pepper in large bowl. Heat 2 tablespoons oil in 10-inch nonstick skillet over medium-high heat until shimmering. Add potato mixture to skillet and reduce heat to medium-low; set bowl aside without washing. Cover potatoes and cook, stirring every 5 minutes, until tender, about 25 minutes.
2. Beat eggs and ½ teaspoon salt together with fork in reserved bowl until thoroughly combined and mixture is pure yellow; do not overbeat. Gently fold in potato mixture, red peppers, and peas, making sure to scrape all of potato mixture out of skillet.
3. Heat remaining 1 teaspoon oil in now-empty skillet over medium-high heat until just smoking. Add egg mixture and cook, shaking skillet and folding mixture constantly for 15 seconds. Smooth top of egg mixture, reduce heat to medium, cover, and cook, gently shaking skillet every 30 seconds, until bottom is golden brown and top is lightly set, about 2 minutes.
4. Off heat, run heat-resistant rubber spatula around edge of skillet and shake skillet gently to loosen tortilla; it should slide around freely in skillet. Slide tortilla onto large plate, then invert onto second large plate and slide back into skillet browned side up. Tuck edges of tortilla into skillet with rubber spatula.
5. Continue to cook over medium heat, gently shaking skillet every 30 seconds, until second side is golden brown, about 2 minutes. Slide tortilla onto cutting board and let cool slightly. Slice and serve hot, warm, or at room temperature.

Honey and Avocado Smoothie

Prep time: 5 minutes | Cook time: 15 minutes | Serves 2

- 1 1/2 cups milk of your choice
- 1 large avocado
- 2 tablespoons honey

1. Add all ingredients to your blender and blend until smooth and creamy.
2. Serve immediately and enjoy!

Peach and Walnut Breakfast Salad

Prep time: 5 minutes | Cook time: 15 minutes | Serves 1

- 1/2 cup low-fat or nonfat cottage cheese, room temperature
- 1 ripe peach, pitted and sliced
- 1/4 cup chopped walnuts, toasted
- 1 teaspoon honey
- 1 tablespoon chopped fresh mint
- Zest of 1 lemon

1. Put the cottage cheese in a small bowl, and top with the peach slices and walnuts.
2. Drizzle with the honey, then top with the fresh mint and a pinch of lemon zest.
3. Serve with a spoon.

Thin-Crust Pizza

Prep time: 5 minutes | Cook time: 35 minutes | Serves 4-6

Dough
- 3 cups (16½ ounces) bread flour
- 2 teaspoons sugar
- ½ teaspoon instant or rapid-rise yeast
- 1⅓ cups ice water
- 1 tablespoon extra-virgin olive oil
- 1½ teaspoons salt
- Sauce and Toppings
- 1 (28-ounce) can whole peeled tomatoes, drained with juice reserved
- 1 tablespoon extra-virgin olive oil
- 2 garlic cloves, minced
- 1 teaspoon red wine vinegar
- 1 teaspoon dried oregano
- ½ teaspoon salt
- ¼ teaspoon pepper
- 1 ounce Parmesan cheese, grated fine (½ cup)
- 8 ounces whole-milk mozzarella cheese, shredded (2 cups)

For the dough
1. Pulse flour, sugar, and yeast in food processor until combined, about 5 pulses. with processor running, slowly add ice water and process until dough is just combined and no dry flour remains, about 10 seconds. Let dough rest for 10 minutes.
2. Add oil and salt to dough and process until dough forms satiny, sticky ball that clears sides of bowl, 30 to 60 seconds. Transfer dough to lightly oiled counter and knead by hand to form smooth, round ball, about 30 seconds. Place dough seam side down in lightly greased large bowl or container, cover tightly with plastic wrap, and refrigerate for at least 24 hours or up to 3 days.

For the sauce and toppings

3. Process tomatoes, oil, garlic, vinegar, oregano, salt, and pepper in clean, dry workbowl until smooth, about 30 seconds. Transfer mixture to 2-cup liquid measuring cup and add reserved tomato juice until sauce measures 2 cups. Reserve 1 cup sauce; set aside remaining sauce for another use.
4. Slide pizza carefully onto baking stone and return oven to 500 degrees. Bake until crust is well browned and cheese is bubbly and partially browned, 8 to 10 minutes, rotating pizza halfway through baking. Transfer pizza to wire rack and let cool for 5 minutes before slicing and serving. Heat broiler for 10 minutes. Repeat with remaining dough, sauce, and toppings, returning oven to 500 degrees when pizza is placed on stone.

Scrambled Eggs with Prosciutto

Prep time: 5 minutes | Cook time: 8 minutes | Serves 6-8

- 3 tablespoons extra-virgin olive oil
- 8 ounces asparagus, trimmed and cut on bias into ¼-inch lengths
- 12 large eggs
- 2 tablespoons water
- ½ teaspoon salt
- ¼ teaspoon pepper
- 2 ounces thinly sliced prosciutto, chopped coarse
- 1 ounce Parmesan cheese, grated (½ cup)

1. Heat 1 tablespoon oil in 12-inch nonstick skillet over medium heat until shimmering. Add asparagus and cook until crisp-tender and lightly browned, 2 to 4 minutes; transfer to bowl and cover to keep warm.
2. Beat eggs, water, salt, and pepper together with fork in bowl until thoroughly combined and mixture is pure yellow; do not overbeat.
3. Wipe skillet clean with paper towels. Heat remaining 2 tablespoons oil in now-empty skillet over medium heat until shimmering. 1½ to 2 minutes.
4. Reduce heat to low and gently but constantly fold eggs until clumped and slightly wet, 30 to 60 seconds. Off heat, gently fold in asparagus, prosciutto, and Parmesan. Serve immediately.

Scrambled Eggs with Potatoes and Harissa

Prep time: 5 minutes | Cook time: 10 minutes | Serves 6-8

- 3 tablespoons extra-virgin olive oil
- 8 ounces red potatoes, unpeeled, cut into ½-inch pieces
- 8 ounces cremini mushrooms, trimmed and halved if small or quartered if large
- ½ onion, chopped fine
- ½ cup plus 2 tablespoons water
- Salt and pepper
- 1 garlic clove, minced
- 12 large eggs
- 2 tablespoons harissa, plus extra for serving
- 2 tablespoons chopped fresh cilantro

1. Heat 1 tablespoon oil in 12-inch nonstick skillet over medium heat until shimmering. Add potatoes, mushrooms, onion, ½ cup water, and ¼ teaspoon salt. Cover and cook, stirring occasionally, until vegetables are softened, 8 to 10 minutes. Uncover and continue to cook, stirring occasionally, until liquid is evaporated and potatoes are golden brown, 3 to 5 minutes. Stir in garlic and cook until fragrant, about 30 seconds; transfer to bowl and cover to keep warm.
2. Beat eggs, ¾ teaspoon salt, ¼ teaspoon pepper, and remaining 2 tablespoons water together with fork in bowl until thoroughly combined and mixture is pure yellow; do not overbeat.
3. Wipe skillet clean with paper towels. Heat remaining 2 tablespoons oil in now-empty skillet over medium heat until shimmering. Add egg mixture and, using heat-resistant rubber spatula, constantly and firmly scrape along bottom and sides of skillet until eggs begin to clump and spatula leaves trail on bottom of skillet, 1½ to 2 minutes.
4. Reduce heat to low and gently but constantly fold eggs until clumped and slightly wet, 30 to 60 seconds. Off heat, gently fold in potato mixture. Drizzle with harissa and sprinkle with cilantro. Serve immediately, passing extra harissa separately.

Za'atar Bread

Prep time: 5 minutes | Cook time: 45 minutes | Serves 6-8

- 3½ cups (19¼ ounces) bread flour
- 2½ teaspoons instant or rapid-rise yeast
- 2½ teaspoons sugar
- 1⅓ cups ice water
- ½ cup plus 2 tablespoons extra-virgin olive oil
- 2 teaspoons salt
- ⅓ cup za'atar
- Coarse sea salt

1. Pulse flour, yeast, and sugar in food processor until combined, about 5 pulses. with processor running, slowly add ice water and process until dough is just combined and no dry flour remains, about 10 seconds. Let dough rest for 10 minutes.
2. Add 2 tablespoons oil and salt to dough and process until dough forms satiny, sticky ball that clears sides of bowl, 30 to 60 seconds. Transfer dough to lightly floured counter and knead by hand to form smooth, round ball, about 30 seconds. Place dough seam side down in lightly greased large bowl or container, cover tightly with plastic wrap, and refrigerate for at least 24 hours or up to 3 days.
3. Remove dough from refrigerator and let sit at room temperature for 1 hour. Coat rimmed baking sheet with 2 tablespoons oil. Gently press down on dough to deflate any large gas pockets. Transfer dough to prepared sheet and, using your fingertips, press out to uniform thickness, taking care not to tear dough. (Dough may not fit snugly into corners.) Cover loosely with greased plastic and let dough rest for 1 hour.
4. Adjust oven rack to lower-middle position and heat oven to 375 degrees. Using your fingertips, gently press dough into corners of sheet and dimple entire surface.
5. Combine remaining 6 tablespoons oil and za'atar in bowl. Using back of spoon, spread oil mixture in even layer on entire surface of dough to edge.
6. Bake until bottom crust is evenly browned and edges are crisp, 20 to 25 minutes, rotating sheet halfway through baking. Let bread cool in sheet for 10 minutes, then transfer to cutting board with spatula. Sprinkle with sea salt, slice, and serve warm.

Savory Breakfast Oats

Prep time: 5 minutes | Cook time: 15 minutes | Serves 2

- 1/2 cup steel-cut oats
- 1 cup water
- 1 large tomato, chopped
- 1 medium cucumber, chopped
- 1 tablespoon olive oil
- Freshly grated, low-fat Parmesan cheese
- Flat-leaf parsley or mint, chopped, for garnish
- Sea salt and freshly ground pepper, to taste

1. Put the oats and 1 cup of water in a medium saucepan and bring to a boil on high heat.
2. Stir continuously until water is absorbed, about 15 minutes.
3. To serve, divide the oatmeal between 2 bowls and top with the tomatoes and cucumber.
4. Drizzle with olive oil, then top with the Parmesan cheese and parsley or mint.
5. Season to taste.
6. Serve immediately.

Scrambled Eggs with Piperade

Prep time: 5 minutes | Cook time 35 minutes | Serves 6-8

- 5 tablespoons extra-virgin olive oil
- 1 large onion, chopped
- 1 bay leaf
- Salt and pepper
- 4 garlic cloves, minced
- 2 teaspoons paprika
- 1 teaspoon minced fresh thyme or ¼ teaspoon dried
- ¾ teaspoon red pepper flakes
- 3 red bell peppers, stemmed, seeded, and cut into ½-inch-wide strips
- 3 tablespoons minced fresh parsley
- 2 teaspoons sherry vinegar
- 12 large eggs
- 2 tablespoons water

1. Heat 3 tablespoons oil in 12-inch nonstick skillet over medium heat until shimmering. Add onion, bay leaf, and ½ teaspoon salt and cook until onion is softened and lightly browned, 5 to 7 minutes. Stir in garlic, paprika, thyme, and pepper flakes and cook until fragrant, about 1 minute. Add bell peppers, Cubanelle peppers, and 1 teaspoon salt, cover, and cook, stirring occasionally, until peppers begin to soften, about 10 minutes.
2. Reduce heat to medium-low. Add tomatoes and reserved juice and cook, uncovered, stirring occasionally, until mixture appears dry and peppers are tender but not mushy, 10 to 12 minutes. Off heat, discard bay leaf. Stir in 2 tablespoons parsley and vinegar and season with salt and pepper to taste; transfer to bowl and cover to keep warm.
3. Reduce heat to low and gently but constantly fold eggs until clumped and slightly wet, 30 to 60 seconds. Off heat, sprinkle with remaining 1 tablespoon parsley and serve immediately with pepper mixture.

Broccoli and Feta Frittata

Prep time: 5 minutes | Cook time: 20 minutes | Serves 6

- 12 large eggs
- ⅓ cup whole milk
- Salt
- 1 tablespoon extra-virgin olive oil
- 12 ounces broccoli florets, cut into ½-inch pieces (3½ to 4 cups)
- Pinch red pepper flakes
- 3 tablespoons water
- ½ teaspoon grated lemon zest plus ½ teaspoon juice
- 4 ounces feta cheese, crumbled into ½-inch pieces (1 cup)

1. Adjust oven rack to middle position and heat oven to 350 degrees. Beat eggs, milk, and ½ teaspoon salt together with fork in bowl until thoroughly combined and mixture is pure yellow; do not overbeat.
2. Add feta and egg mixture and, using heat-resistant rubber spatula, constantly and firmly scrape along bottom and sides of skillet until large curds form and spatula begins to leave trail on bottom of skillet but eggs are still very wet, about 30 seconds. Smooth curds into even layer and let cook without stirring for 30 seconds. Transfer skillet to oven and bake until frittata is slightly puffy and surface bounces back when lightly pressed, 6 to 9 minutes. Using rubber spatula, loosen frittata from skillet and transfer to cutting board. Let sit for 5 minutes before slicing and serving.

Chapter 4

Soups and Small Plates

Old-Fashioned Chicken Soup

Prep time: 5 minutes | Cook time: 40 minutes | Serves 4

- 1 lb chicken breast, boneless, skinless, chopped
- 1 onion, chopped
- 1 carrot, chopped
- 2 small potatoes, peeled, chopped
- 1 tsp cayenne pepper
- 2 egg yolks
- 1 tsp salt
- 3 tbsp lemon juice
- 3 tbsp olive oil
- 4 cups water

1. Add all to the pot, and seal the lid. Set the steam release handle and cook on Soup/Broth mode for 20 minutes on High.
2. Release the pressure naturally, for 10 minutes, open the lid and serve.

Rustic Winter Salad

Prep time: 10 minutes | Cook time: 15 minutes | Serves 4

- 1 small green apple, thinly sliced
- 6 stalks kale, stems removed and greens roughly chopped
- ½ cup crumbled feta cheese
- ½ cup dried currants
- ½ cup chopped pitted kalamata olives
- ½ cup thinly sliced radicchio
- 2 scallions, both green and white parts, thinly sliced
- ¼ cup peeled, julienned carrots
- 2 celery stalks, thinly sliced
- ¼ cup Sweet Red Wine Vinaigrette
- Salt (optional)
- Freshly ground black pepper (optional)

1. In a large bowl, combine the apple, kale, feta, currants, olives, radicchio, scallions, carrots, and celery and mix well.
2. Drizzle with the vinaigrette. Season with salt and pepper (if using), then serve.

Yellow and White Hearts of Palm Salad

Prep time: 10 minutes | Cook time: 15 minutes | Serves 4

- 2 (14-ounce) cans hearts of palm, drained and cut into ½-inch-thick slices
- 1 avocado, cut into ½-inch pieces
- 1 cup halved yellow cherry tomatoes
- ½ small shallot, thinly sliced
- ¼ cup coarsely chopped flat-leaf parsley
- 2 tablespoons low-fat mayonnaise
- 2 tablespoons extra-virgin olive oil
- ¼ teaspoon salt
- ⅛ teaspoon freshly ground black pepper

1. In a large bowl, toss the hearts of palm, avocado, tomatoes, shallot, and parsley.
2. In a small bowl, whisk the mayonnaise, olive oil, salt, and pepper, then mix into the large bowl.

Asparagus Salad

Prep time: 5 minutes | Cook time: 15 minutes | Serves 4

- 1 pound asparagus
- Sea salt and freshly ground pepper, to taste
- 4 tablespoons olive oil
- 1 tablespoon balsamic vinegar
- 1 tablespoon lemon zest

1. Either roast the asparagus or, with a vegetable peeler, shave it into thin strips.
2. Season to taste.
3. Toss with the olive oil and vinegar, garnish with a sprinkle of lemon zest, and serve.

Chorizo Sausage & Fire-Roasted Tomato Soup

Prep time: 5 minutes | Cook time: 30 minutes | Serves 6

- 1 tbsp olive oil
- 2 shallots, chopped
- 3 cloves garlic, minced
- 1 tsp salt
- 4 cups beef broth
- 28 oz fire-roasted diced tomatoes
- ½ cup fresh ripe tomatoes
- 1 tbsp red wine vinegar
- 3 chorizo sausage, chopped
- ½ tsp ground black pepper
- ½ cup thinly chopped fresh basil

1. Warn oil on Sauté and cook chorizo until crispy. Remove to a to a plate lined with paper towel.
2. Add in garlic and onion and cook for 5 minutes until soft. Season with salt. Stir in red wine vinegar, broth, diced tomatoes, sun-dried tomatoes, and black pepper into the cooker.
3. Seal the lid and cook on High Pressure for 8 minutes. Release the ´pressure quickly. Pour the soup into a blender and process until smooth. Divide into bowls, top with chorizo and decorate with basil.

Mushroom and Potato Stew

Prep time: 10 minutes | Cook time: 40 minutes | Serves 6

- 2 tablespoons extra-virgin olive oil
- 5 ounces mushrooms, sliced
- ½ cup diced carrots
- ½ cup diced yellow onion
- ½ cup diced celery
- 2½ cups low-sodium vegetable broth
- 1 cup diced tomatoes
- 1 teaspoon garlic powder
- 1 bay leaf
- 1 russet potato, peeled and finely diced
- 1 cup cooked chickpeas
- ½ cup crumbled feta, for serving

1. In a large sauté pan or skillet, heat the oil over medium heat. Add the mushrooms and cook for 5 minutes, until they reduce in size and soften.
2. Add the carrots, onion, and celery to the pan and cook for 10 minutes, or until the onions are golden. Pour in the vegetable broth, tomatoes, garlic powder, and bay leaf and bring to a simmer. Add the potato.
3. Mix well and cover. Cook for 20 minutes or until the potato is fork-tender.
4. Add in the chickpeas, stir, and the remove the bay leaf. Season with salt and pepper. Serve, topped with feta, and enjoy!

The Mediterranean Diet Cookbook for Beginners

Novara's Bean and Vegetable Soup

Prep time: 10 minutes | Cook time: 25 minutes | Serves 4-6

- ¼ pound pork rind OR fresh side pork (pork belly)
- ⅓ cup vegetable oil
- 1 tablespoon butter
- 2 medium onions, sliced very thin, about 1 cup
- 1 carrot, peeled, washed, and diced
- 1 large stalk of celery, washed and diced
- 2 medium zucchini, washed, then trimmed of both ends and diced
- 1 cup shredded red cabbage
- 1 pound fresh cranberry beans, unshelled weight, OR 1 cup dried cranberry or red kidney beans, soaked and drained but not cooked
- salt
- black pepper, ground fresh from the mill
- 3 cups Basic Homemade Meat Broth, prepared, OR 1 cup canned beef broth diluted with 2 cups water
- freshly grated parmigiano-reggiano cheese for the table

1. Cut the pork into strips about ½ inch long and ¼ inch wide.
2. Put the oil, butter, onion, and pork into a soup pot, and turn on the heat to medium. Stir from time to time.
3. When the onion becomes colored a deep gold, add all the diced vegetables, the shredded cabbage, and the shelled fresh beans or the drained, soaked dried beans. Stir well for about a minute to coat all ingredients thoroughly.
4. Add the cut-up tomatoes with their juice, a pinch of salt, and several grindings of pepper. Stir thoroughly once again, then put in all the broth. If there should not be enough to cover all the ingredients by at least 1 inch, make up the difference with water.
5. If you have made it to serve as a soup and not as a component of la paniscia, ladle it into individual plates or bowls, let it settle a few minutes, and bring to the table along with freshly grated Parmesan.

Creamy Asparagus Soup

Prep time: 5 minutes | Cook time: 40 minutes | Serves 4

- 2 lb fresh asparagus, trimmed, 1-inch thick
- 2 onions, peeled and finely chopped
- 1 cup heavy cream
- 4 cups vegetable broth
- 2 tbsp butter
- 1 tbsp vegetable oil
- ½ tsp salt
- ½ tsp dried oregano
- ½ tsp paprika

1. Warm butter and oil on Sauté. Stir-fry the onions for 2 minutes, until translucent. Add asparagus, oregano, salt, and paprika. Stir well and cook until asparagus soften, for a few minutes.
2. Pour in the broth. Seal the lid and cook on Soup/Broth for 20 minutes on High. Do a quick release and whisk in the heavy cream. Serve chilled or warm.

Sautéed Scallops with Garlic and Parsley

Prep time: 10 minutes | Cook time: 25 minutes | Serves 4

- ½ pound fresh bay scallops OR large sea scallops cut into 3 or 4 pieces
- 2 tablespoons extra virgin olive oil
- 1 teaspoon garlic chopped fine
- salt
- black pepper, ground fresh from the mill
- 1 tablespoon parsley chopped fine
- 1 tablespoon chopped capers
- 2 tablespoons chopped homemade roasted peppers
- 1½ tablespoons fine, dry, unflavored bread crumbs
- 4 scallop shells, available in most cooking equipment shops, OR 4 small gratin dishes

1. Wash the scallops in cold water, drain, and pat thoroughly dry with kitchen towels.
2. Put the olive oil and garlic in a small saucepan; turn on the heat to medium. Cook and stir the garlic until it becomes colored a pale gold, but no darker. Then put in the scallops. Add salt and a few grindings of pepper, and turn up the heat. Cook at a brisk pace, stirring frequently, for a few seconds, until they lose their shiny raw color. Turn off the heat.
3. Preheat the broiler.
4. Add the parsley, capers, chopped peppers, and 1 tablespoon of bread crumbs to the scallops and mix well. Distribute the contents of the pan among the 4 shells or gratin dishes. Sprinkle with the remaining ½ tablespoon of bread crumbs.
5. Run the shells or gratin dishes under the preheated broiler for about 1 minute, or no longer than it takes to form a light brown crust over the scallops. Serve promptly.

Tomato and Pepper Salad

Prep time: 5 minutes | Cook time: 15 minutes | Serves 6

- 3 large yellow peppers
- 1/4 cup olive oil
- 1 small bunch fresh basil leaves
- 2 cloves garlic, minced
- 4 large tomatoes, seeded and diced
- Sea salt and freshly ground pepper, to taste

1. Preheat broiler to high heat and broil the peppers until blackened on all sides.
2. Remove from heat and place in a paper bag. Seal and allow peppers to cool.
3. Once cooled, peel the skins off the peppers, then seed and chop them.
4. Add half of the peppers to a food processor along with the olive oil, basil, and garlic, and pulse several times to make the dressing.
5. Combine the rest of the peppers with the tomatoes and toss with the dressing.
6. Season the salad with sea salt and freshly ground pepper. Allow salad to come to room temperature before serving.

Herby Tomato Soup

Prep time: 10 minutes | Cook time: 10 minutes | Serves 2

- ¼ cup extra-virgin olive oil
- 2 garlic cloves, minced
- 1 (14.5-ounce) can plum tomatoes, whole or diced
- 1 cup vegetable broth
- ¼ cup chopped fresh basil

1. In a medium pot, heat the oil over medium heat, then add the garlic and cook for 2 minutes, until fragrant.
2. Meanwhile, in a bowl using an immersion blender or in a blender, puree the tomatoes and their juices.
3. Add the pureed tomatoes and broth to the pot and mix well. Simmer for 10 to 15 minutes and serve, garnished with basil.

White Bean and Kale Soup

Prep time: 25 minutes | Cook time: 30 minutes | Serves 4

- 1 to 2 tablespoons extra-virgin olive oil
- 1 large shallot, minced
- 1 large purple carrot, chopped
- 1 celery stalk, chopped
- 1 teaspoon garlic powder
- 3 cups low-sodium vegetable broth
- 1 (15-ounce) can cannellini beans
- 1 cup chopped baby kale
- 1 teaspoon salt (optional)
- ½ teaspoon freshly ground black pepper (optional)
- 1 lemon, juiced and zested
- 1½ tablespoons chopped fresh thyme (optional)
- 3 tablespoons chopped fresh oregano (optional)

1. In a large, deep pot, heat the oil. Add the shallot, carrot, celery, and garlic powder and sauté on medium-low heat for 3 to 5 minutes, until the vegetables are golden.
2. Add the vegetable broth and beans and bring to a simmer. Cook for 15 minutes.
3. Add in the kale, salt (if using), and pepper (if using). Cook for another 5 to 10 minutes, until the kale is soft. Right before serving, stir in the lemon juice and zest, thyme (if using), and oregano (if using).

Fig-Pecan Energy Bites

Prep time: 20 minutes | Cook time: 0 minutes | Serves 6

- ¾ cup diced dried figs (6 to 8)
- ½ cup chopped pecans
- ¼ cup rolled oats (old-fashioned or quick oats)
- 2 tablespoons ground flaxseed or wheat germ (flaxseed for gluten-free)
- 2 tablespoons powdered or regular peanut butter
- 2 tablespoons honey

1. In a medium bowl, mix together the figs, pecans, oats, flaxseed, and peanut butter. Drizzle with the honey, and mix everything together. A wooden spoon works well to press the figs and nuts into the honey and powdery ingredients. (If you're using regular peanut butter instead of powdered, the dough will be stickier to handle, so freeze the dough for 5 minutes before making the bites.)
2. Enjoy immediately or chill in the freezer for 5 minutes to firm up the bites before serving. The bites can be stored in a sealed container in the refrigerator for up to 1 week.

Hard-Boiled Eggs with Green Sauce

Prep time: 10 minutes | Cook time: 35 minutes | Serves 6

- 6 extra-large eggs
- 2 tablespoons extra virgin olive oil
- ½ tablespoon chopped capers, soaked and rinsed if packed in salt, drained if in vinegar
- 1 tablespoon chopped parsley
- 3 flat anchovy fillets, chopped very fine
- ¼ teaspoon chopped garlic
- ¼ teaspoon English or Dijon-style mustard
- salt
- a sweet red bell pepper, diced not too fine

1. Put the eggs in cold water and bring to a boil. Cook at a slow boil for 10 minutes, then remove the eggs from the water and set aside to cool.
2. When cool, shell the eggs and cut them in half lengthwise. Carefully scoop out the yolks, taking care to leave the whites intact, and set aside the whites.
3. Put the yolks, olive oil, capers, parsley, anchovies, garlic, mustard, and a tiny pinch of salt in a bowl and, with a fork, mash all the ingredients into a creamy, uniform mixture. (If doing a large quantity for a party, you may want to blend them in a food processor.)
4. Divide the mixture into 12 equal parts and spoon into the cavities of the empty egg whites. Top with cubes of the diced red pepper.

Parsley Garden Vegetable Soup

Prep time: 5 minutes | Cook time: 42 minutes | Serves 8

2 tbsp olive oil
- 1 cup leeks, chopped
- 2 garlic cloves, minced
- 8 cups vegetable stock
- 1 carrot, diced
- 1 potato, diced
- 1 celery stalk, diced
- 1 cup mushrooms
- 1 cup broccoli florets
- 1 cup cauliflower florets
- ½ red bell pepper, diced
- ¼ head green cabbage, chopped
- ½ cup green beans
- ½ salt, or more to taste
- ½ tsp ground black pepper
- ½ cup fresh parsley, chopped

1. Heat oil on Sauté. Add in garlic and onion and cook for 6 minutes until slightly browned. Add in stock, carrot, celery, broccoli, bell pepper, green beans, salt, cabbage, cauliflower, mushrooms, potato, and pepper.
2. Seal lid; cook on High for 6 minutes. Release pressure naturally for about 5 minutes. Stir in parsley and serve.

Double-Apple Spinach Salad

Prep time: 5 minutes | Cook time: 15 minutes | Serves 4

- 8 cups baby spinach
- 1 medium Granny Smith apple, diced
- 1 medium red apple, diced
- 1/2 cup toasted walnuts
- 2 ounces low-fat, sharp white cheddar cheese, cubed
- 3 tablespoons olive oil
- 1 tablespoon red wine vinegar or apple cider vinegar

1. Toss the spinach, apples, walnuts, and cubed cheese together.
2. Lightly drizzle olive oil and vinegar over top and serve.

The Mediterranean Diet Cookbook for Beginners

Riviera Tuna Salad

Prep time: 5 minutes | Cook time: 15 minutes | Serves 4

- 1/4 cup olive oil
- 1/4 cup balsamic vinegar
- 1/2 teaspoon minced garlic
- 1/4 teaspoon dried oregano
- Sea salt and freshly ground pepper, to taste
- 2 tablespoons capers, drained
- 4–6 cups baby greens
- 1 (6-ounce) can solid white albacore tuna, drained
- 1 cup canned garbanzo beans, rinsed and drained
- 1/4 cup low-salt olives, pitted and quartered
- 2 Roma tomatoes, chopped

1. To make the vinaigrette, whisk together the olive oil, balsamic vinegar, garlic, oregano, sea salt, and pepper until emulsified.
2. Stir in the capers. Refrigerate for up to 6 hours before serving.
3. Place the baby greens in a salad bowl or on individual plates, and top with the tuna, beans, olives, and tomatoes.
4. Drizzle the vinaigrette over all, and serve immediately.

Lamb & Spinach Soup

Prep time: 5 minutes | Cook time: 50 minutes | Serves 5

- 1 lb of lamb shoulder, cut into bite-sized pieces
- 10 oz fresh spinach leaves, chopped
- 3 eggs, beaten
- 5 cups vegetable broth
- 3 tbsp olive oil
- 1 tsp salt

1. Place in your instant pot the lamb along with the remaining . Seal the lid, press Soup/Broth and cook for 30 minutes on High Pressure.
2. Do a natural pressure release, for about 10 minutes.

32 | The Mediterranean Diet Cookbook for Beginners

Chapter 5

Rice, Grains and Pasta

Wild Rice and Kale Stuffed Chicken Thighs

Prep time: 10 minutes | Cook time: 22 minutes | Serves 4

- 4 boneless, skinless chicken thighs
- 1 cup cooked wild rice
- ½ cup chopped kale
- 2 garlic cloves, minced
- 1 teaspoon salt
- Juice of 1 lemon
- ½ cup crumbled feta
- Olive oil cooking spray
- 1 tablespoon olive oil

1. Preheat the air fryer to 380°F.
2. Place the chicken thighs between two pieces of plastic wrap, and using a meat mallet or a rolling pin, pound them out to about ¼-inch thick.
3. In a medium bowl, combine the rice, kale, garlic, salt, and lemon juice and mix well.
4. Place a quarter of the rice mixture into the middle of each chicken thigh, then sprinkle 2 tablespoons of feta over the filling.
5. Spray the air fryer basket with olive oil cooking spray.
6. Fold the sides of the chicken thigh over the filling, and then gently place each of them seam-side down into the air fryer basket. Brush each stuffed chicken thigh with olive oil.
7. Roast the stuffed chicken thighs for 12 minutes, then turn them over and cook for an additional 10 minutes, or until the internal temperature reaches 165°F.

Spanish-Style Brothy Rice with Clams and Salsa Verde

Prep time: 5 minutes | Cook time 50 minutes | Serves 4-6

- 5 tablespoons extra-virgin olive oil
- ¼ cup minced fresh parsley
- 6 garlic cloves, minced
- 1 tablespoon white wine vinegar
- 2 cups dry white wine
- 2 pounds littleneck clams, scrubbed
- 5 cups water
- 1 (8-ounce) bottle clam juice
- 1 leek, white and light green parts only, halved lengthwise, chopped fine, and washed thoroughly
- Salt and pepper
- 1½ cups Bomba rice
- Lemon wedges

1. Combine 3 tablespoons oil, parsley, half of garlic, and vinegar in bowl; set aside. Bring wine to boil in large saucepan over high heat. Add clams, cover, and cook, stirring occasionally, until clams open, 5 to 7 minutes.
2. Using slotted spoon, transfer clams to large bowl and cover to keep warm; discard any clams that refuse to open. Stir water and clam juice into wine and bring to simmer. Reduce heat to low, cover, and keep warm.
3. Add 2 cups warm broth and cook, stirring frequently, until almost fully absorbed, about 5 minutes. Continue to cook rice, stirring frequently and adding warm broth, 1 cup at a time, every few minutes as liquid is absorbed, until rice is creamy and cooked through but still somewhat firm in center, 12 to 14 minutes.
4. Off heat, stir in 1 cup warm broth and adjust consistency with extra broth as needed (rice mixture should have thin but creamy consistency; you may have broth left over). Stir in parsley mixture and season with salt and pepper to taste. Nestle clams into rice along with any accumulated juices, cover, and let sit until heated through, 5 to 7 minutes. Serve with lemon wedges.

Toasted Grain and Almond Pilaf

Prep time: 15 minutes | Cook time: 35 minutes | Serves 2

- 1 tablespoon olive oil
- 1 garlic clove, minced
- 3 scallions, minced
- 2 ounces mushrooms, sliced
- ¼ cup sliced almonds
- ½ cup uncooked pearled barley
- 1½ cups low-sodium chicken stock
- ½ teaspoon dried thyme
- 1 tablespoon fresh minced parsley
- Salt

1. Heat the oil in a saucepan over medium-high heat. Add the garlic, scallions, mushrooms, and almonds, and sauté for 3 minutes.
2. Add the barley and cook, stirring, for 1 minute to toast it.
3. Add the chicken stock and thyme and bring the mixture to a boil.
4. Cover and reduce the heat to low. Simmer the barley for 30 minutes, or until the liquid is absorbed and the barley is tender.
5. Sprinkle with fresh parsley and season with salt before serving.

Indoor Paella

Prep time: 10 minutes | Cook time: 75 minutes | Serves 6

- 1 pound extra-large shrimp (21 to 25 per pound), peeled and deveined
- 2 tablespoons extra-virgin olive oil, plus extra as needed
- 8 garlic cloves, minced
- Salt and pepper
- 1 pound boneless, skinless chicken thighs, trimmed and halved crosswise
- 1 red bell pepper, stemmed, seeded, and cut into ½-inch-wide strips
- 8 ounces Spanish-style chorizo sausage, sliced on bias ½ inch thick
- 1 onion, chopped fine
- 1 (14.5-ounce) can diced tomatoes, drained, minced, and drained again
- 2 cups Bomba rice
- 3 cups chicken broth
- ½ teaspoon saffron threads, crumbled
- 1 bay leaf
- 12 mussels, scrubbed and debearded
- ½ cup frozen peas, thawed
- 2 teaspoons chopped fresh parsley
- Lemon wedges

1. Adjust oven rack to lower-middle position and heat oven to 350 degrees. Toss shrimp with 1 tablespoon oil, 1 teaspoon garlic, ¼ teaspoon salt, and ¼ teaspoon pepper in bowl until evenly coated. Cover and refrigerate until needed. Pat chicken dry with paper towels and season with salt and pepper.
2. Heat 2 teaspoons oil in Dutch oven over medium-high heat until shimmering. Add bell pepper and cook, stirring occasionally, until skin begins to blister and turn spotty black, about 4 minutes; transfer to bowl.
3. For optional socarrat, transfer pot to stovetop and remove lid. Cook over medium-high heat for about 5 minutes, rotating pot as needed, until bottom layer of rice is well browned and crisp.
4. Discard any mussels that refuse to open and bay leaf, if it can be easily removed. Arrange bell pepper strips in pinwheel pattern over rice and sprinkle peas over top. Cover and let paella sit for 5 minutes. Sprinkle with parsley and serve with lemon wedges.

Easy Spanish Rice

Prep time: 5 minutes | Cook time: 30 minutes | Serves 4

- 3 tbsp olive oil
- 1 small onion, chopped
- 2 garlic cloves, minced
- 1 serrano pepper, seeded and chopped
- 1 cup bomba rice
- ⅓ cup chunky salsa
- ¼ cup tomato sauce
- ½ cup vegetable broth
- 1 tsp salt
- 1 tbsp chopped fresh parsley

1. Warm oil on Sauté and cook onion, garlic, and serrano pepper for 2 minutes, stirring occasionally until fragrant. Stir in rice, salsa, tomato sauce, vegetable broth, and salt.
2. Seal the lid and cook on High Pressure for 10 minutes. Do a natural pressure release for 10 minutes. Sprinkle with fresh parsley and serve.

Beef-Stuffed Pasta Shells

Prep time: 5 minutes | Cook time: 35 minutes | Serves 4

- 2 tbsp olive oil
- 1 pound ground beef
- 16 ounces pasta shells
- 2 cups water
- 15 ounces tomato sauce
- 15-ounce can black beans, drained and rinsed
- 15-ounces canned corn, drained (or 2 cups frozen corn)
- 10 ounces red enchilada sauce
- 4 ounces diced green chiles
- 1 cup shredded mozzarella cheese
- Salt and ground black pepper to taste
- Additional cheese for topping
- Finely chopped parsley for garnish

1. Heat oil on Sauté. Add ground beef and cook for 7 minutes until it starts to brown.
2. Mix in pasta, tomato sauce, enchilada sauce, black beans, water, corn, and green chiles and stir to coat well. Add more water if desired.
3. Seal the lid and cook on High Pressure for 10 minutes. Do a quick Pressure release. Into the pasta mixture, mix in mozzarella cheese until melted; add black pepper and salt. Garnish with parsley to serve.

Sautéed Cherry Tomato and Fresh Mozzarella Topping

Prep time: 5 minutes | Cook time: 5 minutes | Serves 4-6

- 3 tablespoons extra-virgin olive oil
- 2 garlic cloves, sliced thin
- Pinch sugar
- 1½ pounds cherry tomatoes, halved
- Salt and pepper
- 2 tablespoons shredded fresh basil

1. Cook oil, garlic, pepper flakes, and sugar in 12-inch nonstick skillet over Stir in tomatoes and cook until just beginning to soften, about 1 minute.
2. Season with salt and pepper to taste. Spoon mixture over individual portions of polenta and top with mozzarella and basil. Serve.

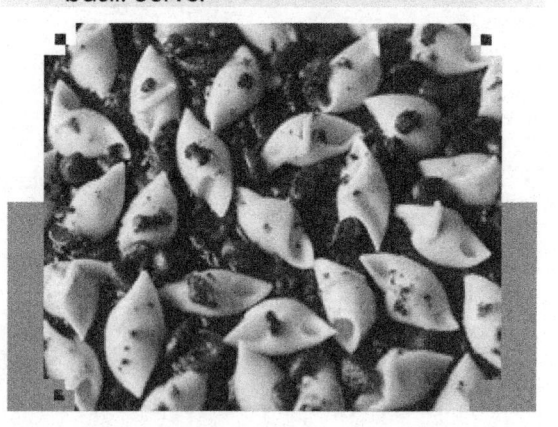

Mediterranean Lentils and Rice

Prep time: 5 minutes | Cook time: 25 minutes| Serves 4

- 2¼ cups low-sodium or no-salt-added vegetable broth
- ½ cup uncooked brown or green lentils
- ½ cup uncooked instant brown rice
- ½ cup diced carrots (about 1 carrot)
- ½ cup diced celery (about 1 stalk)
- ¼ cup diced red onion (about ⅛ onion)
- ¼ cup chopped fresh curly-leaf parsley
- 1½ tablespoons extra-virgin olive oil
- 1 tablespoon freshly squeezed lemon juice (from about ½ small lemon)
- 1 garlic clove, minced (about ½ teaspoon)
- ¼ teaspoon kosher or sea salt
- ¼ teaspoon freshly ground black pepper

1. In a medium saucepan over high heat, bring the broth and lentils to a boil, cover, and lower the heat to medium-low. Cook for 8 minutes.
2. Raise the heat to medium, and stir in the rice. Cover the pot and cook the mixture for 15 minutes, or until the liquid is absorbed. Remove the pot from the heat and let it sit, covered, for 1 minute, then stir.
3. While the lentils and rice are cooking, mix together the carrots, celery, olives, onion, and parsley in a large serving bowl.
4. When the lentils and rice are cooked, add them to the serving bowl. Pour the dressing on top, and mix everything together. Serve warm or cold, or store in a sealed container in the refrigerator for up to 7 days.

PER SERVING

Calories: 170g | Total Fat: 6g | Saturated Fat: 1g | Total Carbs: 25 g | Fiber: 3g | Protein: 5g | Sugar: 3g | Sodium: 566mg |Phosphorus:98 mg | Potassium: 227mg | Cholesterol: 2mg

Pasta Caprese Ricotta-Basil Fusilli

Prep time: 5 minutes | Cook time: 15 minutes | Serves 3

- 1 tbsp olive oil
- 1 onion, thinly chopped
- 6 garlic cloves, minced
- 1 tsp red pepper flakes
- 2 ½ cups dried fusilli
- 1 (15 ounces) can tomato sauce
- 1 cup tomatoes, halved
- 1 cup water
- ¼ cup basil leaves
- 1 tsp salt
- 1 cup Ricotta cheese, crumbled
- 2 tbsp chopped fresh basil

1. Warm oil on Sauté. Add in red pepper flakes, garlic and onion and cook for 3 minutes until soft.
2. Mix in fusilli, tomatoes, half of the basil leaves, water, tomato sauce, and salt. Seal the lid, and cook on High Pressure for 4 minutes. Release the pressure quickly.
3. Transfer the pasta to a serving platter and top with the crumbled ricotta and remaining chopped basil.

Lebanese Rice and Broken Noodles with Cabbage

Prep time: 5 minutes | Cook time: 25 minutes | Serves 6

- 1 tablespoon extra-virgin olive oil
- 1 cup (about 3 ounces) uncooked vermicelli or thin spaghetti, broken into 1- to 1½-inch pieces
- 3 cups shredded cabbage (about half a 14-ounce package of coleslaw mix or half a small head of cabbage)
- 3 cups low-sodium or no-salt-added vegetable broth
- ½ cup water
- 1 cup instant brown rice
- 2 garlic cloves
- ¼ teaspoon kosher or sea salt
- Fresh lemon slices, for serving (optional)

1. In a large saucepan over medium-high heat, heat the oil. Add the pasta and cook for 3 minutes to toast, stirring often. Add the cabbage and cook for 4 minutes, stirring often. Add the broth, water, rice, garlic, salt, and crushed red pepper, and bring to a boil over high heat. Stir, cover, and reduce the heat to medium-low. Simmer for 10 minutes.
2. Remove the pan from the heat, but do not lift the lid. Let sit for 5 minutes. Fish out the garlic cloves, mash them with a fork, then stir the garlic back into the rice. Stir in the cilantro. Serve with the lemon slices (if using).

Grilled Paella

Prep time: 10 minutes | Cook time: 80 minutes | Serves 8

- 1½ pounds boneless, skinless chicken thighs, trimmed and halved crosswise
- Salt and pepper
- 12 ounces jumbo shrimp (16 to 20 per pound), peeled and deveined
- 5 tablespoons extra-virgin olive oil
- 6 garlic cloves, minced
- 1¾ teaspoons hot smoked paprika
- 3 tablespoons tomato paste
- 1 pound littleneck clams, scrubbed
- 8 ounces Spanish-style chorizo sausage, cut into ½-inch pieces
- 1 cup frozen peas, thawed
- Lemon wedges

1. Pat chicken dry with paper towels and season both sides with 1 teaspoon salt and 1 teaspoon pepper. Toss shrimp with 1½ teaspoons oil, ½ teaspoon garlic, ¼ teaspoon paprika, and ¼ teaspoon salt in bowl until evenly coated. Set aside.
2. FOR A CHARCOAL GRILL Open bottom vent completely. Light large chimney starter mounded with charcoal briquettes (7 quarts). When top coals are partially covered with ash, pour evenly over grill. Using tongs, arrange 20 unlit briquettes evenly over coals. Set cooking grate in place, cover, and open lid vent completely. Heat grill until hot, about 5 minutes.
3. FOR A GAS GRILL Turn all burners to high, cover, and heat grill until hot, about 15 minutes. Leave all burners on high.
4. Sprinkle peas evenly over paella, cover grill, and cook until liquid is fully absorbed and rice on bottom of pan sizzles, 5 to 8 minutes. Continue to cook, uncovered, checking frequently, until uniform golden-brown crust forms on bottom of pan, 8 to 15 minutes longer. (Rotate and slide pan around grill as necessary to ensure even crust formation.) Remove from grill, cover with aluminum foil, and let sit for 10 minutes. Serve with lemon wedges.

Rice & Olives Stuffed Mushrooms

Prep time: 5 minutes | Cook time: 45 minutes | Serves 4

- 4 large portobello mushrooms, stems and gills removed
- 2 tbsp melted butter
- ½ cup brown rice, cooked
- 1 tomato, seed removed and chopped
- ¼ cup black olives, pitted and chopped
- 1 green bell pepper, seeded and diced
- ½ cup feta cheese, crumbled
- Juice of 1 lemon
- ½ tsp salt
- ½ tsp ground black pepper
- Minced fresh cilantro, for garnish
- 1 cup vegetable broth

1. Brush the mushrooms with butter. Arrange the mushrooms in a single layer in an oiled baking pan. In a bowl, mix the rice, tomato, olives, bell pepper, feta cheese, lemon juice, salt, and black pepper.
2. Spoon the rice mixture into the mushrooms. Pour in the broth, seal the lid and cook on High Pressure for 10 minutes. Do a quick release. Garnish with fresh cilantro and serve immediately.

Creamy Parmesan Polenta

Prep time: 5 minutes | Cook time 35 minutes | Serves 4-6

- 7½ cups water
- Salt and pepper
- Pinch baking soda
- 1½ cups coarse-ground cornmeal
- 2 ounces Parmesan cheese, grated (1 cup), plus extra for serving
- 2 tablespoons extra-virgin olive oil

1. Bring water to boil in large saucepan over medium-high heat. Stir in 1½ teaspoons salt and baking soda. Slowly pour cornmeal into water in steady stream while stirring back and forth with wooden spoon or rubber spatula. Bring mixture to boil, stirring constantly, about 1 minute. Reduce heat to lowest setting and cover.
2. After 5 minutes, whisk polenta to smooth out any lumps that may have formed, about 15 seconds. (Make sure to scrape down sides and bottom of saucepan.) Cover and continue to cook, without stirring, until polenta grains are tender but slightly al dente, about 25 minutes longer. (Polenta should be loose and barely hold its shape; it will continue to thicken as it cools.)
3. Off heat, stir in Parmesan and oil and season with pepper to taste. Cover and let sit for 5 minutes. Serve, passing extra Parmesan separately.

Chili-Garlic Rice with Halloumi

Prep time: 5 minutes | Cook time: 20 minutes | Serves 6

- 2 cups water
- 2 tbsp brown sugar
- 2 tbsp rice vinegar
- 1 tbsp sweet chili sauce
- 1 tbsp olive oil
- 1 tsp fresh minced garlic
- 20 ounces Halloumi cheese, cubed
- 1 cup rice
- ¼ cup chopped fresh chives, for garnish

1. Heat the oil on Sauté and fry the halloumi for 5 minutes until golden brown. Set aside.
2. Split the rice between bowls. Top with fried halloumi and sprinkle with fresh chives before serving.

Pasta Shells Filled with Ricotta & Spinach

Prep time: 5 minutes | Cook time: 1 hour | Serves 6

- 2 cups onion, chopped
- 1 cup carrot, chopped
- 3 garlic cloves, minced
- 3 ½ tbsp olive oil,
- 1 (28 ounces) canned tomatoes, crushed
- 12 ounces conchiglie pasta
- 1 tbsp olive oil
- Salt and ground black pepper to taste
- 1 cup shredded cheddar cheese

1. Warm olive oil on Sauté. Add in onion, carrot, and garlic, and cook for 5 minutes until tender. Stir in tomatoes and cook for another 10 minutes. Remove to a bowl and set aside.
2. Wipe the pot with a damp cloth, add pasta and cover with enough water. Seal the lid and cook for 5 minutes on High Pressure. Do a quick release and drain the pasta. Lightly Grease olive oil to a baking sheet.
3. Pour 1 cup of water in the pot of the Pressure cooker and insert the trivet. Lower the baking dish onto the trivet. Seal the lid, and cook for 15 minutes on High Pressure. Do a quick release. Take away the foil. Place the stuffed shells to serving plates and top with tomato sauce before serving.

Creamy Chicken Pasta with Pesto Sauce

Prep time: 5 minutes | Cook time: 30 minutes | Serves 8

- 3½ cups water
- 4 chicken breast, boneless, skinless, cubed
- 8 oz macaroni pasta
- 1 tbsp butter
- 1 tablespoon salt, divided
- 2 cups fresh collard greens, trimmed
- 1 cup cherry tomatoes, halved
- ½ cup basil pesto sauce
- ¼ cup cream cheese, at room temperature
- 1 garlic clove, minced
- 1 tsp freshly ground black pepper to taste
- ¼ cup Asiago cheese, grated
- Freshly chopped basil for garnish

1. Add water, chicken, 2 tsp salt, butter, and macaroni, and stir well to mix and be submerged in water.
2. Press Cancel, open the lid, get rid of ¼ cup water from the pot.
3. Set on Sauté mode. Into the pot, mix in collard greens, pesto sauce, garlic, remaining 1 teaspoon salt, cream cheese, tomatoes, and black pepper. Cook, for 1 to 2 minutes as you stir, until sauce is creamy. Place the pasta into serving plates. Top with asiago cheese and basil before serving.

Chapter 6

Poultry

Lebanese Grilled Chicken

Prep time: 5 minutes | Cook time: 15 minutes | Serves 4

- 1/2 cup olive oil
- 1/4 cup apple cider vinegar
- Zest and juice of 1 lemon
- 4 cloves garlic, minced
- 2 teaspoons sea salt
- 1 teaspoon Arabic 7 spices (baharaat)
- 1/2 teaspoon cinnamon
- 1 chicken, cut into 8 pieces

1. Combine all the ingredients except the chicken in a shallow dish or plastic bag.
2. Place the chicken in the bag or dish and marinate overnight, or at least for several hours.
3. Drain, reserving the marinade. Heat the grill to medium-high.
4. Cook the chicken pieces for 10–14 minutes, brushing them with the marinade every 5 minutes or so.
5. The chicken is done when the crust is golden brown and an instant-read thermometer reads 180 degrees in the thickest parts. Remove skin before eating.

Beans with Chicken Sausage and Escarole

Prep time: 5 minutes | Cook time: 4 hours | Serves 6

- 12 ounces chicken sausage, cut into ¼-inch rounds
- 1 15-ounce can cannellini beans, drained and rinsed
- 1 15-ounce can chickpeas, drained and rinsed
- 1 28-ounce can whole tomatoes, drained and chopped
- 1½ cups chicken stock
- 1 bay leaf
- 1 teaspoon dried thyme
- ¼ teaspoon red pepper flakes
- ½ teaspoon sea salt
- ¼ teaspoon black pepper
- 1 small head escarole, chopped
- ¼ Cup coarsely grated parmigiano-reggiano cheese
- 2 tablespoons chopped fresh flat-leaf parsley

1. Combine sausage, cannellini beans, chickpeas, tomatoes, and stock in the slow cooker. Sprinkle on the bay leaf, thyme, red pepper flakes, ½ teaspoon salt, and ¼ teaspoon pepper.
2. Cover and cook on low for 4 hours.
3. Stir in the escarole and cook an additional 5 to 8 minutes, until just wilted. Stir in the Parmigiano-Reggiano and parsley. Season with additional sea salt and black pepper. Serve hot.

Spinach and Chicken Pita Pizza

Prep time: 5 minutes | Cook time 7 minutes | Serves 1

- 1 whole wheat pita
- 1 tablespoon olive oil
- 1 garlic clove, minced
- ¼ teaspoon red pepper flakes
- ½ cup baby spinach
- ¼ sliced red onion
- ½ cup cooked chicken breast, cubed
- ¼ cup feta cheese, crumbled

1. Preheat the air fryer to 380°F.
2. Brush the top of the pita with the olive oil and top with the garlic, red pepper flakes, spinach, onion, chicken, and feta.
3. Place the pizza into the air fryer basket and cook for 7 minutes.
4. Remove the pizza from the air fryer. Cut into 2 to 4 pieces and enjoy!

Herbed Roasted Chicken

Prep time: 15 minutes | Cook time: 1 hour | Serves 7

- 3 garlic cloves, minced
- 1 (5-pounds) whole chicken
- 1 teaspoon fresh lemon zest, finely grated
- 1 teaspoon dried thyme, crushed
- 1 teaspoon dried oregano, crushed
- 1 teaspoon dried rosemary, crushed
- 1 teaspoon smoked paprika
- 2 tablespoons fresh lemon juice
- 2 tablespoons olive oil
- Salt and ground black pepper

1. In a bowl, mix the garlic, lemon zest, herbs, and spices.
2. Rub the chicken evenly with the herb mixture.
3. Drizzle the chicken with lemon juice and oil. Set aside at room temperature for about 2 hours.
4. Set the temperature of the Air Fryer to 360 degrees F. Grease the Air Fryer basket.
5. Place chicken into the prepared Air Fryer basket, breast side down. Air Fry for about 50 minutes.
6. Flip the chicken and Air Fry for about 10 more minutes.
7. Remove from the Air Fryer and place chicken onto a cutting board for about 10 minutes before carving.

Breaded Turkey Cutlets

Prep time: 5 minutes | Cook time: 8 minutes | Serves 4

- ½ cup whole wheat bread crumbs
- ¼ teaspoon paprika
- ¼ teaspoon salt
- ¼ teaspoon black pepper
- ⅛ teaspoon dried sage
- ⅛ teaspoon garlic powder
- 1 egg
- 4 turkey breast cutlets
- Chopped fresh parsley, for serving

1. Preheat the air fryer to 380°F.
2. In a medium shallow bowl, whisk together the bread crumbs, paprika, salt, black pepper, sage, and garlic powder.
3. In a separate medium shallow bowl, whisk the egg until frothy.
4. Dip each turkey cutlet into the egg mixture, then into the bread crumb mixture, coating the outside with the crumbs. Place the breaded turkey cutlets in a single layer in the bottom of the air fryer basket, making sure that they don't touch each other.
5. Bake for 4 minutes. Turn the cutlets over, then bake for 4 minutes more, or until the internal temperature reaches 165°F. Sprinkle on the parsley and serve.

The Mediterranean Diet Cookbook for Beginners

Lemon and Paprika Herb-Marinated Chicken

Prep time: 10 minutes, plus 30 minutes to marinate | Cook time: 15 minutes | Serves 2

- 2 tablespoons olive oil
- 4 tablespoons freshly squeezed lemon juice
- ¼ teaspoon salt
- 1 teaspoon paprika
- 1 teaspoon dried basil
- ½ teaspoon dried thyme
- ¼ teaspoon garlic powder
- 2 (4-ounce) boneless, skinless chicken breasts

1. In a bowl with a lid, combine the olive oil, lemon juice, salt, paprika, basil, thyme, and garlic powder.
2. Add the chicken and marinate for at least 30 minutes, or up to 4 hours.
3. When ready to cook, heat the grill to medium-high (about 350–400°F) and oil the grill grate. Alternately, you can also cook these in a nonstick sauté pan over medium-high heat.
4. Grill the chicken for 6 to 7 minutes, or until it lifts away from the grill easily. Flip it over and grill for another 6 to 7 minutes, or until it reaches an internal temperature of 165°F.

Chicken with Potatoes

Prep time: 15 minutes | Cook time: 1 hour | Serves 2

- 1 (1½-pounds) whole chicken
- 1 tablespoon olive oil
- ½ pound of small potatoes
- Salt and ground black pepper

1. Set the temperature of the Air Fryer to 390 degrees F. Grease the Air Fryer basket.
2. Season the chicken with salt and pepper.
3. Place chicken into the prepared Air Fryer basket and cook for about 40 minutes. Transfer the chicken onto a plate and cover with a piece of foil to keep warm.
4. Add the potatoes, oil, salt, and black pepper in a bowl and toss to coat well.
5. Again, set the temperature of the Air Fryer to 390 degrees F. Grease the Air Fryer basket.
6. Place the potatoes into the prepared Air Fryer basket. Air Fry for about 20 minutes or until golden brown. Remove from the Air Fryer and transfer potatoes into a bowl.
7. Cut the chicken into desired pieces and serve alongside the potatoes.

Chicken Sausage Cassoulet

Prep time: 5 minutes | Cook time: 7 to 8 hours | Serves 6

- Nonstick cooking oil spray
- 1 large yellow onion, chopped
- ¾ Cup baby carrots, halved lengthwise
- 2 tablespoons garlic, minced
- 1¼ pounds chicken or turkey sausage, cut into 2-inch sections
- Two 8-ounce cans tomato sauce
- 1 tablespoon dried herbes de provence
- 1 teaspoon black pepper
- Two 15-ounce cans great northern beans, drained and rinsed
- 4 slices bacon, cooked and crumbled

1. Coat the inside of the slow cooker crock with cooking oil spray. Add the onion, carrots, garlic, sausage, and tomato sauce. Sprinkle with the herbes de Provence and pepper. Stir to combine.
2. Cover and cook on low for 7 to 8 hours or high for 3½ to 4 hours. Add the beans to the pot in the last hour of cooking.
3. Serve hot, with bacon sprinkled on each serving.

Braised Duck with Fennel Root

Prep time: 5 minutes | Cook time: 15 minutes | Serves 6

- 1/4 cup olive oil
- 1 whole duck, cleaned
- 3 teaspoon fresh rosemary
- 2 garlic cloves, minced
- Sea salt and freshly ground pepper, to taste
- 3 fennel bulbs, cut into chunks
- 1/2 cup sherry

1. Preheat the oven to 375 degrees.
2. Heat the olive oil in a large stew pot or Dutch oven.
3. Season the duck, including the cavity, with the rosemary, garlic, sea salt, and freshly ground pepper.
4. Place the duck in the oil, and cook it for 10–15 minutes, turning as necessary to brown all sides.
5. Add the fennel bulbs and cook an additional 5 minutes.
6. Pour the sherry over the duck and fennel, cover the pot, and cook in the oven for 30–45 minutes, or until internal temperature of the duck is 140–150 degrees at its thickest part.
7. Allow duck to sit for 15 minutes before serving.

Chicken Shawarma

Prep time: 10 minutes | Cook time 15 minutes | Serves 4

- 1 pound boneless skinless chicken breasts, cubed
- 1/4 cup nonfat plain Greek yogurt
- 2 tablespoons olive oil
- 1 teaspoon dried oregano
- 1 teaspoon ground cumin
- 1 teaspoon ground cinnamon
- 1 teaspoon salt
- 1/4 teaspoon ground turmeric
- 1/4 teaspoon black pepper
- Rice, for serving (optional)
- Greek salad, for serving (optional)
- Tzatziki sauce, for serving (optional)

1. Preheat the air fryer to 380°F.
2. In a large bowl, combine all ingredients and mix together until the chicken is coated well.
3. Spread the chicken mixture in an even layer in the air fryer basket, then cook for 10 minutes. Stir the chicken mixture and cook for an additional 5 minutes.
4. Serve with rice, a Greek salad, and tzatziki sauce.

Lemon-Pepper Chicken Thighs

Prep time: 5 minutes | Cook time 22 minutes | Serves 4

- 4 bone-in chicken thighs, skin and fat removed
- 2 tablespoons olive oil
- 1 teaspoon garlic powder
- Black pepper
- 1 lemon, sliced

1. Preheat the air fryer to 380°F.
2. Coat the chicken thighs in the olive oil, garlic powder, and salt.
3. Tear off four pieces of aluminum foil, with each sheet being large enough to envelop one chicken thigh.
4. Place one chicken thigh onto each piece of foil, season it with black pepper, and then top it with slices of lemon.
5. Bake for 20 to 22 minutes, or until the internal temperature of the chicken has reached 165°F.
6. Remove the foil packets from the air fryer. Carefully open each packet to avoid a steam burn.

Chicken Fricassee with Red Cabbage

Prep time: 10 minutes | Cook time: 25 minutes | Serves 4

- 1 cup onion sliced very thin
- ¼ cup extra virgin olive oil plus 1 tablespoon
- 2 garlic cloves, peeled and each cut into 4 pieces
- salt
- a 3- to 4-pound chicken, cut into 8 pieces
- ½ cup dry red wine
- black pepper, ground fresh from the mill

1. Put the sliced onion, the ¼ cup oil, and the garlic in a sauté pan, turn the heat on to medium, and cook the garlic until it becomes colored a deep gold. Add the shredded cabbage. Stir thoroughly to coat well, sprinkle with salt, stir again, adjust heat to cook at a gentle simmer, and put a lid on the pan. Cook the cabbage for 40 minutes or more, turning it over from time to time, until it has become very tender and considerably reduced in bulk.
2. Wash the chicken pieces in cold water, and pat thoroughly dry with cloth or paper towels.
3. In another pan, put in 1 tablespoon of olive oil, turn on the heat to medium, and, after warming up the oil very briefly, put in all the chicken pieces skin side down in a single layer. Turn the chicken after a little while to brown the pieces equally on both sides, then transfer them to the other pan, all except the breast, which you'll hold aside until later. Turn the chicken over in the cabbage, add the wine and a few grindings of pepper, cover the pan, putting the lid on slightly ajar, and continue cooking at a slow, steady simmer. From time to time turn the chicken pieces over, sprinkling them once with salt. After 40 minutes add the breasts. Cook for about 10 minutes more, until the chicken is tender all the way through and the meat comes easily off the bone. You will no longer be able to recognize the cabbage as such; it will have become a dark, supple sauce for the chicken. Transfer the entire contents of the pan to a warm platter and serve at once.

Marinated Chicken

Prep time: 5 minutes | Cook time: 15 minutes | Serves 4

- 1/2 cup olive oil
- 2 tablespoon fresh rosemary
- 1 teaspoon minced garlic
- Juice and zest of 1 lemon
- 1/4 cup chopped flat-leaf parsley
- Sea salt and freshly ground pepper, to taste
- 4 boneless, skinless chicken breasts

1. Mix all ingredients except the chicken together in a plastic bag or bowl.
2. Place the chicken in the container and shake/stir so the marinade thoroughly coats the chicken.
3. Refrigerate up to 24 hours.
4. Heat a grill to medium heat and cook the chicken for 6–8 minutes a side. Turn only once during the cooking process.
5. Serve with a Greek salad and brown rice.

Chicken Cacciatora

Prep time: 10 minutes | **Cook time:** 25 minutes | Serves 4-6

- 3- to 4-pound chicken, cut into 6 to 8 pieces
- 2 tablespoons extra virgin olive oil
- 1 cup onion sliced very thin
- 2 garlic cloves, peeled and sliced very thin
- salt
- black pepper, ground fresh from the mill
- ⅓ cup dry white wine
- 1½ cups fresh, very ripe, firm meaty tomatoes, skinned raw with a peeler and chopped, OR canned imported italian plum tomatoes, cut up, with their juice

1. Wash the chicken in cold water and pat thoroughly dry with cloth or paper towels.
2. Choose a sauté pan that can subsequently contain all the chicken pieces without crowding them. Put in the olive oil and the sliced onion, and turn on the heat to medium. Cook the onion, turning it occasionally, until it becomes translucent.
3. Add the sliced garlic and the chicken pieces, putting them in skin side facing down. Cook until the skin forms a golden crust, then turn the pieces and do the other side.
4. Add the cut-up tomatoes, turn down the heat to cook at an intermittent simmer, and cover the pan, putting the lid on slightly askew. Turn and baste the chicken pieces from time to time while they are cooking. Whenever you find that the liquid in the pan becomes insufficient, add 2 tablespoons of water. Cook until the chicken thighs feel very tender when prodded with a fork, and the meat comes easily off the bone, about 40 minutes.

Skillet Creamy Tarragon Chicken and Mushrooms

Prep time: 10 minutes | **Cook time:** 20 minutes | Serves 2

- 2 tablespoons olive oil, divided
- ½ medium onion, minced
- 4 ounces baby bella (cremini) mushrooms, sliced
- 2 small garlic cloves, minced
- 2 teaspoons tomato paste
- 2 teaspoons dried tarragon
- 2 cups low-sodium chicken stock
- 6 ounces pappardelle pasta
- ¼ cup plain full-fat Greek yogurt
- Salt
- Freshly ground black pepper

1. Heat 1 tablespoon of the olive oil in a sauté pan over medium-high heat. Add the onion and mushrooms and sauté for 5 minutes. Add the garlic and cook for 1 minute more.
2. Move the vegetables to the edges of the pan and add the remaining 1 tablespoon of olive oil to the center of the pan. Place the cutlets in the center and let them cook for about 3 minutes, or until they lift up easily and are golden brown on the bottom.
3. Flip the chicken and cook for another 3 minutes.
4. Mix in the tomato paste and tarragon. Add the chicken stock and stir well to combine everything. Bring the stock to a boil.
5. Add the pappardelle. Break up the pasta if needed to fit into the pan. Stir the noodles so they don't stick to the bottom of the pan.
6. The sauce will tighten up as it cools, so if it seems too thick, add a few tablespoons of water.

Lemon-Garlic Chicken

Prep time: 2 hours' minutes | Cook time: 35 minutes | Serves 4

- Lemon juice ¼ cup
- 1 Tbsp. olive oil
- 1 tsp mustard
- Cloves of garlic
- ¼ tsp salt
- ⅛ tsp black pepper
- Chicken thighs
- Lemon wedges

1. In a bowl, whisk together the lemon juice, olive oil, mustard, garlic, salt, and pepper.
2. Place the chicken thighs in a Ziploc bag. Spill marinade over the chicken and seal the bag, ensuring all chicken parts are covered. Cool for at least 2 hours.
3. Preheat the Air Fryer to 360°F.
4. Remove the chicken with towels from the marinade, and pat dry. Place the chicken pieces in the Air Fryer basket and cook them in batches.
5. Fry for 24 minutes till the chicken is no longer pink. Upon serving, press a lemon slice across each piece.

Sheet Pan Pesto Chicken with Crispy Garlic Potatoes

Prep time: 15 minutes | Cook time: 50 minutes | Serves 2

- 12 ounces small red potatoes (3 or 4 potatoes)
- 1 tablespoon olive oil
- ¼ teaspoon salt
- ½ teaspoon garlic powder
- 1 (8-ounce) boneless, skinless chicken breast
- 3 tablespoons prepared pesto

1. Preheat the oven to 425°F and set the rack to the bottom position. Line a baking sheet with parchment paper. (Do not use foil, as the potatoes will stick.)
2. Scrub the potatoes and dry them well, then dice into 1-inch pieces.
3. Check the potatoes to make sure they are golden brown on the top and bottom. Toss them again and add the chicken breast to the pan.
4. Turn the heat down to 350°F and let the chicken and potatoes roast for 30 minutes. Check to make sure the chicken reaches an internal temperature of 165°F and the potatoes are tender inside.

Chicken and Potato Tagine

Prep time: 5 minutes | Cook time: 15 minutes | Serves 6

- 1 chicken, cut up into 8 pieces
- 1 medium onion, thinly sliced
- 3 cloves garlic, minced
- 1/4 cup olive oil
- 1/2 teaspoon ground cumin
- 1/2 teaspoon freshly ground pepper
- 1/4 teaspoon ginger
- 1 teaspoon paprika
- Sea salt, to taste
- 3 cups potatoes, peeled and diced
- 1/2 cup flat-leaf parsley, chopped
- 1/2 cup fresh cilantro, chopped
- 1 cup fresh or frozen green peas

1. Place the chicken, onion, garlic, olive oil, and seasonings into a Dutch oven. Add about 2 cups water and bring to a boil over medium-high heat. Reduce heat and cover. Simmer for 30 minutes.
2. Add the potatoes, parsley, and cilantro, and simmer an additional 20 minutes, or until the potatoes are almost tender.
3. Add the peas at the last moment, simmering for an additional 5 minutes. Serve hot.

Chapter 7

Pork, Beef and Lamb

Potato, Swiss Chard, and Lamb Hash

Prep time: 5 minutes | Cook time 45 minutes | Serves 4

- 1½ pounds russet potatoes, peeled and cut into ½-inch pieces
- 2 tablespoons extra-virgin olive oil
- Salt and pepper
- 1½ pounds Swiss chard, stems sliced ¼ inch thick, leaves sliced into ½-inch-wide strips
- 8 ounces ground lamb
- 1 onion, chopped fine
- 3 garlic cloves, minced
- 2 teaspoons paprika
- 1 teaspoon ground cumin
- 1 teaspoon ground coriander
- ¼ teaspoon cayenne pepper
- 4 large eggs
- 1 tablespoon minced fresh chives

1. Toss potatoes with 1 tablespoon oil, ½ teaspoon salt, and ¼ teaspoon pepper in bowl. Cover and microwave until potatoes are translucent around edges, 7 to 9 minutes, stirring halfway through microwaving; drain well.
2. Heat remaining 1 tablespoon oil in 12-inch nonstick skillet over medium-high heat until shimmering. Add chard stems and ¼ teaspoon salt and cook until softened and lightly browned, 5 to 7 minutes. Stir in chard leaves, 1 handful at a time, and cook until mostly wilted, about 4 minutes; transfer to bowl with potatoes.
3. Cook lamb in now-empty skillet over medium-high heat, breaking up meat with wooden spoon, until beginning to brown, about 5 minutes. Stir in onion and cook until softened and lightly browned, 5 to 7 minutes. Stir in garlic, paprika, cumin, coriander, and cayenne and cook until fragrant, about 30 seconds.
4. Stir in chard-potato mixture. Using back of spatula, gently pack chard-potato mixture into skillet and cook, without stirring, for 2 minutes. Flip hash, 1 portion at a time, and lightly repack into skillet. Repeat flipping process every few minutes until potatoes are well browned, 6 to 8 minutes.
5. Off heat, make 4 shallow indentations (about 2 inches wide) in surface of hash using back of spoon, pushing hash up into center and around edges of skillet (bottom of skillet should be exposed in each divot). Crack 1 egg into each indentation and season with salt and pepper. Cover and cook over medium-low heat until whites are just set and yolks are still runny, 4 to 6 minutes. Sprinkle with chives and serve immediately.

Beef Ragù

Prep time: 10 minutes | Cook time: 4 hours 30 minutes | Serves 6

- 1 medium yellow onion, diced small
- 3 cloves garlic, minced
- 6 tablespoons tomato paste
- 3 tablespoons chopped fresh oregano leaves (or 3 teaspoons dried oregano)
- One 4-pound beef chuck roast, halved
- Coarse sea salt
- Black pepper
- 2 cups beef stock
- 2 tablespoons red wine vinegar

1. Combine the onion, garlic, tomato paste, and oregano in the slow cooker.
2. Season the roast halves with salt and pepper and place on top of the onion mixture in the slow cooker. Add the beef stock.
3. Cover and cook until meat is tender and can easily be pulled apart with a fork, on high for 4½ hours, or on low for 9 hours. Let cool 10 minutes.
4. Shred the meat while it is still in the slow cooker using two forks. Stir the vinegar into the sauce. Serve hot, over pasta.

Beef Roast Braised with Onions

Prep time: 10 minutes | Cook time: 25 minutes | Serves 4-6

- ¼ pound pancetta OR salt pork in a single piece
- 2 pounds boneless beef roast, preferably the brisket
- 5 cloves
- 4 medium onions sliced very, very thin
- salt
- black pepper, ground fresh from the mill

1. Preheat oven to 325°.
2. Cut the pancetta or salt pork into narrow strips about ¼ inch wide. Use half the strips to lard the meat with a larding needle, or by an alternative method as suggested in the introductory remarks above.
3. Choose a heavy-bottomed pot just large enough to accommodate the roast snugly. Spread the sliced onion on the bottom of the pot, over it distribute the remaining strips of pancetta or salt pork, then put in the meat. Season liberally with salt and pepper, and cover tightly. If the lid does not provide a tight fit, place a sheet of aluminum foil between it and the pot. Put on the uppermost rack of the preheated oven.
4. Cook for about 3½ hours, until the meat feels very tender when prodded with a fork. Turn the roast after the first 30 minutes, and every 30 to 40 minutes thereafter. You will find that the color of the meat is dull and unlovely at first, but as it finishes cooking and the onions become colored a dark brown it develops a rich, dark patina.
5. When done, slice the meat and arrange the slices on a warm platter. Pour the contents of the pan and the juices left on the cutting board over the meat, and serve at once.

Beef Tenderloin with Red Wine

Prep time: 10 minutes | Cook time: 25 minutes | Serves 4

- 3 garlic cloves
- 1 tablespoon vegetable oil
- 2 tablespoons butter
- 4 beef fillets, cut 1 inch thick
- ⅔ cup flour, spread on a plate
- salt
- black pepper, ground fresh from the mill
- ⅔ cup full-bodied dry red wine (follow suggestions in wine note to recipe pot roast of beef braised in red wine)

1. Lightly mash the garlic cloves with a knife handle, just hard enough to split the peel, which you will loosen and discard.
2. Choose a sauté pan that can later accommodate the 4 fillets without overlapping. Put in the oil and butter, and turn on the heat to medium high.
3. Dredge both sides of the meat in flour. As soon as the butter foam begins to subside, put in the fillets and the mashed garlic cloves. Brown the meat deeply on both sides, then transfer to a plate, using a slotted spoon or spatula. Season with salt and liberal grindings of pepper.
4. Add the wine to the pan and let it boil away completely while using a wooden spoon to loosen the cooking residues on the bottom and sides of the pan. When the wine has boiled away, return the fillets to the pan. Cook them in the pan juices for about 1 minute on each side, then transfer the fillets with all the cooking juices to a warm platter, and serve at once.

Yogurt-and-Herb-Marinated Pork Tenderloin

Prep time: 5 minutes | Cook time: 25 minutes| Serves 6

- Nonstick cooking spray
- 2 medium pork tenderloins (10 to 12 ounces each)
- ½ teaspoon freshly ground black pepper
- ½ teaspoon kosher or sea salt
- ¼ cup 2% plain Greek yogurt
- 1 tablespoon chopped fresh rosemary
- Tzatziki yogurt sauce from Chickpea Patties in Pitas (here, step 3) or store-bought tzatziki sauce

1. Preheat the oven to 500°F.
2. Line a large, rimmed baking sheet with aluminum foil. Place a wire cooling rack on the aluminum foil, and spray the rack with nonstick cooking spray.
3. Place both pieces of the pork on the wire rack, folding under any skinny ends of the meat to ensure even cooking. Sprinkle both pieces evenly with the pepper and salt.
4. In a small bowl, mix together the yogurt and rosemary. Using a spoon or your fingers, slather the yogurt mixture over all sides of the pork.
5. Roast on the wire rack for 10 minutes. Remove the baking sheet from the oven, and turn over both pieces of pork. Roast for 10 to 12 minutes more, or until the internal temperature of the pork measures 145°F on a meat thermometer and the juices run clear. Remove the pork from the rack and place on a clean cutting board. Let rest for 5 minutes, then slice.
6. While the pork is roasting, make the tzatziki yogurt sauce, adding fresh mint to the sauce, if desired. Serve the sauce with the pork.

Pork & Mushroom Stew

Prep time: 5 minutes | Cook time: 50 minutes | Serves 2

- 2 pork chops, bones removed and cut into pieces
- 1 cup crimini mushrooms, chopped
- 2 large carrots, chopped
- ½ tsp garlic powder
- 1 tsp salt
- ½ black pepper
- 2 tbsp butter
- 1 cup beef broth
- 1 tbsp apple cider vinegar
- 2 tbsp cornstarch

1. Season the meat with salt and pepper. Add butter and pork chops to the pot and brown for 10 minutes, stirring occasionally, on Sauté mode. Add mushrooms and cook for 5 minutes.
2. Add the remaining and seal the lid. Cook on High Pressure for 25 minutes. Do a quick release and serve hot.

Fennel Pork Estofado

Prep time: 5 minutes | Cook time: 40 minutes | Serves 4

- 12 oz pork neck, cut into bite-sized pieces
- 2 tbsp flour
- 1 tbsp fennel seeds, crushed
- 4 tbsp vegetable oil
- 2 onions, peeled, chopped
- 1 carrot
- A handful of chopped celery
- 10 oz button mushrooms
- 4 cups beef broth
- 1 chili pepper, chopped
- 1 tbsp cayenne pepper

1. Heat oil on Sauté. Add onions and cook for 2 minutes, until translucent. Add flour, chili pepper, carrot, celery, cayenne pepper, and fennel seeds, and continue cooking for 2 more minutes, stirring constantly.
2. Press Cancel, and add meat, mushrooms, beef broth, and water. Seal the lid and cook on Manual/Pressure Cook mode for 30 minutes on High Pressure. Do a quick release and serve immediately.

Beef Brisket with Onions

Prep time: 10 minutes | Cook time: 6 hours | Serves 6

- 1 large yellow onion, thinly sliced
- 2 garlic cloves, smashed and peeled
- 1 first cut of beef brisket (4 pounds), trimmed of excess fat
- Coarse sea salt
- Black pepper
- 2 cups chicken broth
- 2 tablespoons chopped fresh parsley leaves, for serving

1. Combine the onion and garlic in the slow cooker.
2. Season the brisket with salt and pepper, and place, fat-side up, in the slow cooker.
3. Add the broth to the slow cooker. Cover and cook until the brisket is fork-tender, on high for about 6 hours.
4. Remove the brisket to a cutting board and thinly slice across the grain.
5. Serve with the onion and some cooking liquid, sprinkled with parsley.

Pressure Cooker Moroccan Pot Roast

Prep time: 15 minutes | Cook time: 50 minutes | Serves 4

- 8 ounces mushrooms, sliced
- 4 tablespoons extra-virgin olive oil
- 3 small onions, cut into 2-inch pieces
- 2 tablespoons paprika
- 1½ tablespoons garam masala
- 2 teaspoons salt
- ¼ teaspoon ground white pepper
- 2 tablespoons tomato paste
- 1 small eggplant, peeled and diced
- 1¼ cups low-sodium beef broth
- ½ cup halved apricots
- ⅓ cup golden raisins
- 3 pounds beef chuck roast
- 2 tablespoons honey
- 1 tablespoon dried mint
- 2 cups cooked brown rice

1. Set an electric pressure cooker to Sauté and put the mushrooms and oil in the cooker. Sauté for 5 minutes, then add the onions, paprika, garam masala, salt, and white pepper. Stir in the tomato paste and continue to sauté.
2. Add the eggplant and sauté for 5 more minutes, until softened. Pour in the broth. Add the apricots and raisins. Sear the meat for 2 minutes on each side.
3. Close and lock the lid and set the pressure cooker to high for 50 minutes.
4. When cooking is complete, quick release the pressure. Carefully remove the lid, then remove the meat from the sauce and break it into pieces. While the meat is removed, stir honey and mint into the sauce.
5. Assemble plates with ½ cup of brown rice, ½ cup of pot roast sauce, and 3 to 5 pieces of pot roast.

Pan-Roasted Lamb with Juniper Berries

Prep time: 10 minutes | Cook time: 25 minutes | Serves 4

- 2½ pounds lamb shoulder, cut into 3- to 4-inch pieces, with the bone in
- 1 tablespoon chopped carrot
- 2 tablespoons chopped onion
- 1 tablespoon chopped celery
- 1 cup dry white wine
- 2 garlic cloves, mashed lightly with a knife handle, the skin removed
- a sprig of fresh rosemary OR ½ teaspoon chopped dried
- 1½ teaspoons lightly crushed juniper berries
- salt
- black pepper, ground fresh from the mill

1. Choose a heavy-bottomed or enameled cast-iron pot that will contain all the ingredients. Put all the ingredients into it, cover the pot, and turn the heat on to medium low. Turn the lamb pieces over about twice an hour.
2. After 2 hours, the ingredients should have shed a considerable amount of juice. Set the pot's cover on slightly ajar, and continue cooking at slightly higher heat. Turn the meat from time to time. After an hour and a half more, the lamb should feel very tender when prodded with a fork. If there is still too much liquid in the pot, uncover, raise the heat, and reduce it to a less runny consistency. Taste the meat and correct for salt.
3. Tip the pot and spoon off as much of the liquefied lamb fat as you can. Transfer the entire contents of the pot to a warm platter and serve at once.

Mediterranean Lamb Bowl

Prep time: 15 minutes | Cook time: 15 minutes | Serves 2

- 2 tablespoons extra-virgin olive oil
- ¼ cup diced yellow onion
- 1 pound ground lamb
- 1 teaspoon dried mint
- 1 teaspoon dried parsley
- ½ teaspoon red pepper flakes
- ¼ teaspoon garlic powder
- 1 cup cooked rice
- ½ teaspoon za'atar seasoning
- ½ cup halved cherry tomatoes
- 1 cucumber, peeled and diced
- 1 cup store-bought hummus or Garlic-Lemon Hummus
- 1 cup crumbled feta cheese
- 2 pita breads, warmed (optional)

1. In a large sauté pan or skillet, heat the olive oil over medium heat and cook the onion for about 2 minutes, until fragrant. Add the lamb and mix well, breaking up the meat as you cook. Once the lamb is halfway cooked, add mint, parsley, red pepper flakes, and garlic powder.
2. In a medium bowl, mix together the cooked rice and za'atar, then divide between individual serving bowls. Add the seasoned lamb, then top the bowls with the tomatoes, cucumber, hummus, feta, and pita (if using).

Herb-Roasted Beef Tips with Onions

Prep time: 5 minutes | Cook time: 10 minutes | Serves 4

- 1 pound rib eye steak, cubed
- 2 garlic cloves, minced
- 2 tablespoons olive oil
- 1 tablespoon fresh oregano
- 1 teaspoon salt
- ½ teaspoon black pepper
- 1 yellow onion, thinly sliced

1. Preheat the air fryer to 380°F.
2. In a medium bowl, combine the steak, garlic, olive oil, oregano, salt, pepper, and onion. Mix until all of the beef and onion are well coated.
3. Put the seasoned steak mixture into the air fryer basket. Roast for 5 minutes. Stir and roast for 5 minutes more.
4. Let rest for 5 minutes before serving with some favorite sides.

Shawarma Pork Tenderloin with Pitas

Prep time: 15 minutes | Cook time: 35 minutes | Serves 8

For The Shawarma Spice Rub:
- 1 teaspoon ground cumin
- 1 teaspoon ground coriander
- 1 teaspoon ground turmeric
- ¾ teaspoon sweet Spanish paprika
- ½ teaspoon ground cloves
- ¼ teaspoon salt
- ¼ teaspoon freshly ground black pepper
- ⅛ teaspoon ground cinnamon

For The Shawarma:
- 1½ pounds pork tenderloin
- 3 tablespoons extra-virgin olive oil
- 1 tablespoon garlic powder
- Salt
- Freshly ground black pepper
- 1½ tablespoons Shawarma Spice Rub
- 4 pita pockets, halved, for serving
- 1 to 2 tomatoes, sliced, for serving
- ¼ cup Pickled Onions, for serving
- ¼ cup Pickled Turnips, for serving
- ¼ cup store-bought hummus or Garlic-Lemon Hummus

To Make The Shawarma Seasoning:
1. In a small bowl, combine the cumin, coriander, turmeric, paprika, cloves, salt, pepper, and cinnamon and set aside.

To Make The Shawarma:
2. Preheat the oven to 400°F.
3. Put the pork tenderloin on a plate and cover with olive oil and garlic powder on each side. Season with salt and pepper and rub each side of the tenderloin with a generous amount of shawarma spices.
4. Place the pork tenderloin in the center of a roasting pan and roast for 20 minutes per pound, or until the meat begins to bounce back as you poke it. If it feels like there's still fluid under the skin, continue cooking. Check every 5 to 7 minutes until it reaches the desired tenderness and juices run clear.
5. Remove the pork from the oven and let rest for 10 minutes.
6. Serve the pork tenderloin shawarma with pita pockets, tomatoes, Pickled Onions (if using), Pickled Turnips (if using), and hummus.

Beef and Goat Cheese Stuffed Peppers

Prep time: 10 minutes | Cook time 30 minutes | Serves 4

- 1 pound lean ground beef
- ½ cup cooked brown rice
- 2 Roma tomatoes, diced
- 3 garlic cloves, minced
- ½ yellow onion, diced
- 2 tablespoons fresh oregano, chopped
- 1 teaspoon salt
- ½ teaspoon black pepper
- ¼ teaspoon ground allspice
- 4 ounces goat cheese
- ¼ cup fresh parsley, chopped

1. Preheat the air fryer to 360°F.
2. In a large bowl, combine the ground beef, rice, tomatoes, garlic, onion, oregano, salt, pepper, and allspice. Mix well.
3. Divide the beef mixture equally into the halved bell peppers and top each with about 1 ounce (a quarter of the total) of the goat cheese.
4. Place the peppers into the air fryer basket in a single layer, making sure that they don't touch each other. Bake for 30 minutes.
5. Remove the peppers from the air fryer and top with fresh parsley before serving.

Thin Lamb Chops Fried in Parmesan Batter

Prep time: 10 minutes | Cook time: 35 minutes | Serves 6

- 12 single-rib lamb chops, partly boned and flattened as described above
- ½ cup freshly grated parmigiano-reggiano cheese, spread on a plate
- 2 eggs, beaten lightly in a deep dish
- 1 cup fine, dry, unflavored bread crumbs, spread on a plate
- vegetable oil
- salt
- black pepper, ground fresh from the mill

1. Turn the chops on both sides in the grated Parmesan, pressing the chop firmly against the crumbs, using the palm of your hand to cause the cheese to adhere well to the meat. Tap the chops gently against the plate to shake off excess cheese.
2. Dip them into the beaten egg, letting excess egg flow back into the dish. Then turn the chops in the bread crumbs, coating both sides, and tap them again to shake off excess.
3. Pour enough oil in a skillet to come ¼ inch up the sides, and turn on the heat to medium. When the oil is very hot, slip as many chops into the pan as will fit without crowding. As soon as one side forms a nice, golden crust, sprinkle it with salt and pepper, turn the chop, and sprinkle salt and pepper on the other side.
4. As soon as the second side has formed a crust transfer to a warm platter, using a slotted spoon or spatula. Repeat the procedure, slipping more chops into the pan as soon as there is room for them. When all the chops are done serve promptly.

Italian Tomato Glazes Pork Meatloaf

Prep time: 5 minutes | Cook time: 30 minutes | Serves 4

For the Meatloaf:
- 2 pounds ground pork
- 2 garlic cloves, minced
- 1 cup breadcrumbs
- 1 large-sized egg
- 1 cup milk
- 2 small onions, finely chopped
- Salt and cracked black pepper, to taste
- ½ tsp turmeric powder
- ½ tsp dried oregano
- Cooking spray, for greasing

For the Topping:
- 1 cup ketchup
- 2 tbsp brown sugar
- ¼ cup tomato paste
- 1 tsp garlic powder
- ½ tsp onion powder
- ½ tsp cayenne Pepper

1. Place the trivet at the bottom of your pressure cooker and pour 1 cup of water. Lightly grease a round sheet pan, that fits in your pressure cooker.
2. Mix ground pork, bread crumbs, milk, onion, egg, salt, black pepper, oregano, and thyme in a mixing bowl. Use your hands to combine thoroughly. Shape into a loaf and place onto the prepared sheet pan.
3. In another bowl, mix the for the topping. Spread the topping over the meatloaf and lower the sheet pan onto the trivet. Seal the lid, select Pressure Cook and cook for 24 minutes at High.
4. Once ready, do a quick pressure release. Remove to a cutting board and slice before serving.

Lamb Burger

Prep time: 15 minutes | Cook time: 15 minutes | Serves 4

- 1 pound ground lamb
- ½ small red onion, grated
- 1 tablespoon dried parsley
- 1 teaspoon dried oregano
- 1 teaspoon ground cumin
- 1 teaspoon garlic powder
- ½ teaspoon dried mint
- ¼ teaspoon paprika
- ¼ teaspoon kosher salt
- ⅛ teaspoon freshly ground black pepper
- Extra-virgin olive oil, for panfrying
- 4 pita breads, for serving (optional)
- Tzatziki Sauce, for serving (optional)
- Pickled Onions, for serving (optional)

1. In a bowl, combine the lamb, onion, parsley, oregano, cumin, garlic powder, mint, paprika, salt, and pepper. Divide the meat into 4 small balls and work into smooth discs.
2. In a large sauté pan or skillet, heat a drizzle of olive oil over medium heat or brush a grill with oil and set it to medium. Cook the patties for 4 to 5 minutes on each side, until cooked through and juices run clear.
3. Enjoy lamb burgers in pitas, topped with tzatziki sauce and pickled onions (if using).

Egyptian Eggah with Ground Beef and Spinach

Prep time: 5 minutes | Cook time 25 minutes | Serves 4-6

- 8 ounces (8 cups) baby spinach
- 6 tablespoons water
- 4 teaspoons extra-virgin olive oil
- 1 pound leeks, whites and light green parts only, halved lengthwise, sliced thin, and washed thoroughly
- 8 ounces 90 percent lean ground beef
- 1 garlic clove, minced
- 1 teaspoon ground cumin
- ¼ teaspoon ground cinnamon
- Salt and pepper
- 8 large eggs
- ¼ cup minced fresh cilantro

1. Place spinach and ¼ cup water in large bowl, cover, and microwave until spinach is wilted and decreased in volume by about half, about 5 minutes. Remove bowl from microwave and keep covered for 1 minute. Transfer spinach to colander and gently press to release liquid. Transfer spinach to cutting board and chop coarse. Return to colander and press again.
2. Heat 1 teaspoon oil in 10-inch nonstick skillet over medium heat until shimmering. Add leeks and cook until softened, about 5 minutes. Add ground beef and cook, breaking up meat with wooden spoon, until beginning to brown, 5 to 7 minutes. Stir in garlic, cumin, cinnamon, ½ teaspoon salt, and ¼ teaspoon pepper and cook until fragrant, about 30 seconds. Stir in spinach until heated through, about 1 minute; transfer to bowl and let cool slightly.
3. Beat eggs, remaining 2 tablespoons water, ½ teaspoon salt, and ¼ teaspoon pepper together with fork in large bowl until thoroughly combined and mixture is pure yellow; do not overbeat. Gently fold in spinach mixture and cilantro, making sure to scrape all of spinach mixture out of skillet.
4. Heat remaining 1 tablespoon oil in now-empty skillet over medium-high heat until just smoking. Add egg mixture and cook, shaking skillet and folding mixture constantly for 15 seconds. Smooth top of egg mixture, reduce heat to medium, cover, and cook, gently shaking skillet every 30 seconds, until bottom is golden brown and top is lightly set, about 3 minutes.
5. Off heat, run heat-resistant rubber spatula around edge of skillet and shake skillet gently to loosen eggah; it should slide around freely in skillet. Slide eggah onto large plate, then invert onto second large plate and slide back into skillet browned side up. Tuck edges of eggah into skillet with rubber spatula. Continue to cook over medium heat, gently shaking skillet every 30 seconds, until second side is golden brown, about 2 minutes. Slide eggah onto cutting board and let cool slightly. Slice and serve hot, warm, or at room temperature.

Chapter 8

Fish and Seafood

Herbed Garlic Shrimp

Prep time: 5 minutes | Cook time: 15 minutes | Serves 4

- 1 pound shrimp, peeled and deveined
- ½ cup olive oil
- 1 tsp garlic powder
- 1 tsp dried rosemary, crushed
- ½ tsp dried basil
- ½ tsp dried sage
- ½ tsp salt
- 1 tsp chili pepper

1. Pour 1 ½ cups of water in the inner pot. In a bowl, mix oil, garlic, rosemary, basil, sage, salt, and chili. Brush the marinade over shrimp.
2. Insert the steamer rack, and arrange the shrimp on top. Seal the lid and cook on Steam for 3 minutes on High. Release the steam naturally, for 10 minutes.
3. Press Sauté and stir-fry for 2 more minutes, or until golden brown.

Pan-Roasted Wild Cod with Tomatoes

Prep time: 10 minutes | Cook time: 20 minutes | Serves 2

- 1 tablespoon olive oil
- ½ medium onion, minced
- 2 garlic cloves, minced
- 1 teaspoon oregano
- 1 (15-ounce) can diced tomatoes with basil
- 1 (15-ounce) can artichoke hearts in water, drained and halved
- ¼ cup pitted Greek olives, drained
- 10 ounces wild cod (2 smaller pieces may fit better in the pan)
- Salt
- Freshly ground black pepper

1. Heat olive oil in a sauté pan over medium-high heat. Add the onion and sauté for about 10 minutes, or until golden. Add the garlic and oregano and cook for another 30 seconds.
2. Mix in the tomatoes, artichoke hearts, and olives.
3. Place the cod on top of the vegetables. Cover the pan and cook for 10 minutes, or until the fish is opaque and flakes apart easily. Season with salt and pepper.

Lemon Garlic Shrimp in Air Fryer

Prep time: 5 minutes | Cook time: 10 minutes | Serves 2

- Olive oil: 1 Tbsp.
- Small shrimp: 4 cups, peeled, tails removed
- One lemon juice and zest
- Parsley: 1/4 cup sliced
- Red pepper flakes (crushed): 1 pinch
- Four cloves of grated garlic
- Sea salt: 1/4 teaspoon

1. Preheat the Air Fryer to 400 °F.
2. Mix olive oil, lemon zest, red pepper flakes, shrimp, kosher salt, and garlic in a bowl and coat the shrimp well.
3. Place shrimp in the Air Fryer basket and coat with oil spray.
4. Cook at 400°F for 8 minutes. Toss the shrimp halfway through.
5. Serve with lemon slices and parsley.

Shrimp with Tomatoes and Chili Pepper

Prep time: 10 minutes | Cook time: 25 minutes | Serves 4-6

- ¼ cup extra virgin olive oil
- 3 tablespoons chopped onion
- 2 teaspoons chopped garlic
- chopped hot red chili pepper, to taste
- 3 tablespoons chopped parsley
- 1⅔ cups canned imported Italian plum tomatoes, cut up, with their juice (see fresh tomato note below)
- salt
- Grilled or oven-browned slices of crusty bread

1. Put the olive oil and onion in a sauté pan, turn on the heat to medium, and cook the onion until it becomes translucent. Add the garlic and chopped chili pepper. When the garlic becomes colored a pale gold, add the parsley, stir once or twice, then add the cut-up tomatoes with their juice together with liberal pinches of salt. Stir thoroughly to coat the tomatoes well, and adjust heat to cook at a steady simmer. Stir from time to time and cook for about 20 minutes, until the oil floats free from the tomatoes.
2. Shell the shrimp and remove their dark vein. If they are larger than medium size, split them in half lengthwise. Wash in several changes of cold water, then pat thoroughly dry with paper towels.
3. Add the shrimp to the simmering sauce, turning them 2 or 3 times to coat them well. Cover the pan and cook for about 2 to 3 minutes, depending on the thickness of the shrimp. Taste and correct for salt and chili pepper. Serve at once with crusty bread to dunk in the sauce.

Sea Bass with Roasted Root Vegetables

Prep time: 10 minutes | Cook time 15 minutes | Serves 4

- 1 carrot, diced small
- 1 parsnip, diced small
- 1 rutabaga, diced small
- ¼ cup olive oil
- 2 teaspoons salt, divided
- 4 sea bass fillets
- ½ teaspoon onion powder
- 2 garlic cloves, minced
- 1 lemon, sliced, plus additional wedges for serving

1. Preheat the air fryer to 380°F.
2. In a small bowl, toss the carrot, parsnip, and rutabaga with olive oil and 1 teaspoon salt.
3. Lightly season the sea bass with the remaining 1 teaspoon of salt and the onion powder, then place it into the air fryer basket in a single layer.
4. Spread the garlic over the top of each fillet, then cover with lemon slices.
5. Pour the prepared vegetables into the basket around and on top of the fish. Roast for 15 minutes.
6. Serve with additional lemon wedges if desired.

Steamed Cod with Garlic and Swiss Chard

Prep time: 5 minutes | Cook time 12 minutes | Serves 4

- 1 teaspoon salt
- ½ teaspoon dried oregano
- ½ teaspoon dried thyme
- ½ teaspoon garlic powder
- 4 cod fillets
- ½ white onion, thinly sliced
- 2 cups Swiss chard, washed, stemmed, and torn into pieces
- ¼ cup olive oil
- 1 lemon, quartered

1. Preheat the air fryer to 380°F.
2. In a small bowl, whisk together the salt, oregano, thyme, and garlic powder.
3. Tear off four pieces of aluminum foil, with each sheet being large enough to envelop one cod fillet and a quarter of the vegetables.
4. Place a cod fillet in the middle of each sheet of foil, then sprinkle on all sides with the spice mixture.
5. In each foil packet, place a quarter of the onion slices and ½ cup Swiss chard, then drizzle 1 tablespoon olive oil and squeeze ¼ lemon over the contents of each foil packet.
6. Fold and seal the sides of the foil packets and then place them into the air fryer basket. Steam for 12 minutes.
7. Remove from the basket, and carefully open each packet to avoid a steam burn.

Summer Mackerel Niçoise Platter

Prep time: 10 minutes | Cook time: 15 minutes | Serves 2

For The Dressing:
- 3 tablespoons red wine vinegar
- 4 tablespoons olive oil
- 1 teaspoon Dijon mustard
- ¼ teaspoon salt
- Pinch freshly ground black pepper

For The Salad:
- 2 teaspoons salt
- 2 small red potatoes
- 1 cup tender green beans
- 2 cups baby greens
- 2 hard-boiled eggs
- ½ cup cherry tomatoes, halved
- ⅓ cup Niçoise olives
- 2 (4-ounce) tins of mackerel fillets, drained

To Make The Dressing:
1. Combine the vinegar, olive oil, Dijon mustard, salt, and pepper in a lidded jar. Shake or whisk the dressing until thoroughly combined. Taste and add more salt and pepper to taste, if needed.

To Make The Salad:
7. Fill a large saucepan with about 3 inches of water, add salt, and bring to a boil. Add the potatoes and cook for 10 to 15 minutes, or until you can pierce them with a sharp knife, but they are still firm.
8. Remove the potatoes and add the green beans to the water. Reduce the heat and let the beans simmer for 5 minutes.
9. Place both the potatoes and green beans in a colander and run it under cold water until vegetables are cool.
10. Lay the baby greens on a large platter.
11. Slice the potatoes and arrange them on one section of the platter. Add the green beans to another section of the platter. Slice the hard-boiled eggs and arrange them in another section.
12. Continue with the tomatoes, olives, and mackerel fillets. Pour the dressing over the salad.

No-Mayo Florence Tuna Salad

Prep time: 10 minutes | **Cook time:** 15 minutes | Serves 4

- 4 cups spring mix greens
- 1 (15-ounce) can cannellini beans, drained
- 2 (5-ounce) cans water-packed, white albacore tuna, drained (I prefer Wild Planet brand)
- ⅔ cup crumbled feta cheese
- ½ cup thinly sliced sun-dried tomatoes
- ¼ cup sliced pitted kalamata olives
- ¼ cup thinly sliced scallions, both green and white parts
- 3 tablespoons extra-virgin olive oil
- ½ teaspoon dried cilantro
- 2 or 3 leaves thinly chopped fresh sweet basil
- 1 lime, zested and juiced
- Kosher salt
- Freshly ground black pepper

1. In a large bowl, combine greens, beans, tuna, feta, tomatoes, olives, scallions, olive oil, cilantro, basil, and lime juice and zest. Season with salt and pepper, mix, and enjoy!

Juicy Air Fryer Salmon

Prep time: 5 mins **Cook time:** 12 minutes | Serves 4

- Lemon pepper seasoning: 2 teaspoons
- Salmon: 4 cups
- Olive oil: one tablespoon
- Seafood seasoning: 2 teaspoons
- Half lemon's juice
- Garlic powder: 1 teaspoon
- Salt to taste

1. In a bowl, add one tbsp. of olive oil and half lemon juice.
2. Pour this mixture over salmon and rub. Leave the skin on salmon. It will come off when cooked.
3. Rub the salmon with salt and spices.
4. Put parchment paper in the air fryer basket. Put the salmon in the Air Fryer.
5. Cook at 360 F for ten minutes. Cook until inner salmon temperature reaches 140 F.
6. Let the salmon rest five minutes before serving. Serve with lemon wedges.

Herbed Shrimp Pita

Prep time: 5 minutes | **Cook time** 8 minutes | Serves 4

- 1 pound medium shrimp, peeled and deveined
- 2 tablespoons olive oil
- 1 teaspoon dried oregano
- ½ teaspoon dried thyme
- ½ teaspoon garlic powder
- ¼ teaspoon onion powder
- ½ teaspoon salt
- ¼ teaspoon black pepper
- 4 whole wheat pitas
- 4 ounces feta cheese, crumbled
- 1 cup shredded lettuce
- 1 tomato, diced
- ¼ cup black olives, sliced
- 1 lemon

1. Preheat the oven to 380°F.
2. In a medium bowl, combine the shrimp with the olive oil, oregano, thyme, garlic powder, onion powder, salt, and black pepper.
3. Pour shrimp in a single layer in the air fryer basket and cook for 6 to 8 minutes, or until cooked through.
4. Remove from the air fryer and divide into warmed pitas with feta, lettuce, tomato, olives, and a squeeze of lemon.

Tomatoes Stuffed with Shrimp

Prep time: 10 minutes | Cook time: 35 minutes | Serves 6

- 6 large, round, ripe firm tomatoes
- salt
- 1 tablespoon red wine vinegar
- ¾ pound small raw shrimp in the shell
- Mayonnaise, made as directed on , using the yolk of 1 large egg, ½ cup vegetable oil, and 2½ to 3 tablespoons freshly squeezed lemon juice
- 1½ tablespoons capers, soaked and rinsed if packed in salt, drained if packed in vinegar
- 1 teaspoon English or Dijon-style mustard
- parsley

1. Slice the tops off the tomatoes. with a small spoon, possibly a serrated grapefruit spoon, scoop out all the seeds, and remove some of the dividing walls, leaving 3 or 4 large sections. Don't squeeze the tomato at any time. Sprinkle with salt, and turn the tomatoes upside down on a platter to let excess liquid drain out.
2. Rinse the shrimp in cold water. Fill a pot with 2 quarts of water. Add the vinegar and 1 tablespoon of salt, and bring to a boil. Drop in the shrimp and cook for just 1 minute (or more, depending on their size) after the water returns to a boil. Drain, shell, and devein the shrimp. Set aside to cool completely.
3. Shake off the excess liquid from the tomatoes without squeezing them. Stuff to the top with the shrimp mixture. Garnish each tomato with a whole shrimp and 1 or 2 parsley leaves. Serve at room temperature or even just slightly chilled.

Shrimp Ceviche Salad

Prep time: 15 minutes | Cook time:5 minutes |Serves 4

- 1 pound fresh shrimp, peeled and deveined
- 1 small red or yellow bell pepper, cut into ½-inch chunks
- ½ English cucumber, peeled and cut into ½-inch chunks
- ½ small red onion, cut into thin slivers
- ¼ cup chopped fresh cilantro or flat-leaf Italian parsley
- ⅓ cup freshly squeezed lime juice
- 2 tablespoons freshly squeezed lemon juice
- ½ cup extra-virgin olive oil
- 1 teaspoon salt
- ½ teaspoon freshly ground black pepper
- 2 ripe avocados, peeled, pitted, and cut into ½-inch chunks

1. Cut the shrimp in half lengthwise. In a large glass bowl, combine the shrimp, bell pepper, cucumber, onion, and cilantro.
2. In a small bowl, whisk together the lime, lemon, and clementine juices, olive oil, salt, and pepper. Pour the mixture over the shrimp and veggies and toss to coat. Cover and refrigerate for at least 2 hours, or up to 8 hours. Give the mixture a toss every 30 minutes for the first 2 hours to make sure all the shrimp "cook" in the juices.
3. Add the cut avocado just before serving and toss to combine.

Sweet and Sour Tuna Steaks

Prep time: 10 minutes | Cook time: 35 minutes | Serves 6

- 2½ pounds fresh tuna, cut into ½-inch-thick steaks
- 3 cups onion sliced very, very thin
- ⅓ cup extra virgin olive oil
- salt
- 1 cup flour, spread on a plate
- black pepper, ground fresh from the mill
- 2 teaspoons granulated sugar
- ¼ cup red wine vinegar
- ⅓ cup dry white wine
- 2 tablespoons chopped parsley

1. Remove the skin circling the tuna steaks, wash them in cold water, and pat thoroughly dry with paper towels.
2. Choose a sauté pan broad enough to accommodate later all the steaks in a single layer without overlapping. Put in the sliced onion, 2 tablespoons of olive oil, 1 or 2 large pinches of salt, and turn on the heat to medium low. Cook until the onion has wilted completely, then turn up the heat to medium and continue cooking, stirring from time to time, until the onion becomes colored a deep golden brown.
3. Using a slotted spoon or spatula, transfer the onion to a small bowl. Add the remaining 2 tablespoons of olive oil to the pan, turn the heat up to medium high, dredge the tuna steaks in flour on both sides, and slip them into the pan. Cook them for 2 to 3 minutes, depending on their thickness, then sprinkle with salt and pepper, add the sugar, vinegar, wine, and onions, turn the heat up to high, and cover the pan. Cook at high heat for about 2 minutes, uncover the pan, add the parsley, turn the fish steaks over once or twice, then transfer them to a warm serving platter.
4. If there are thin juices left in the pan, boil them down and at the same time scrape loose with a wooden spoon any cooking residue sticking to the bottom. If, on the other hand, there is no liquid in the pan, add 2 tablespoons of water and boil it away while loosening the cooking residues. Pour the contents of the pan over the tuna, and serve at once.

Parmesan Shrimp

Prep time: 5 minutes | Cook time: 10 minutes | Serves 4

- 2 tablespoons olive oil
- 8 cups, peeled, deveined jumbo cooked shrimp
- 2/3 cup (grated) parmesan cheese
- 1 teaspoon onion powder
- 1 teaspoon pepper
- four cloves of minced garlic
- 1/2 teaspoon oregano
- 1 teaspoon basil
- lemon wedges

1. Mix parmesan cheese, onion powder, oregano, olive oil, garlic, basil, and pepper in a bowl. Coat the shrimp in this mixture.
2. Spray oil on the Air Fryer basket and put shrimp in it. Cook for ten minutes at 350°F.
3. Drizzle the lemon on the shrimp before serving.

Roasted Salmon with Fennel Salad

Prep time: 15 minutes | Cook time:10 minutes | Serves 4

- Skinless and center-cut: 4 salmon fillets
- Lemon juice: 1 teaspoon (fresh)
- Parsley: 2 teaspoons (chopped)
- Salt: 1 teaspoon, divided
- Olive oil: 2 tablespoons
- Chopped thyme: 1 teaspoon
- Fennel heads: 4 cups (thinly sliced)
- One clove of minced garlic
- Fresh dill: 2 tablespoons, chopped
- Orange juice: 2 tablespoons (fresh)
- Greek yogurt: 2/3 cup (reduced-| Fat:)

1. In a bowl, add half teaspoon of salt, parsley, and thyme, mix well. Rub oil over salmon, and sprinkle with thyme mixture.
2. Put salmon fillets in the Air Fryer basket, and cook for ten minutes at 350°F.
3. In the meantime, mix garlic, fennel, orange juice, yogurt, half tsp. of salt, dill, and lemon juice in a bowl.
4. Serve the roasted salmon with fennel salad.

Tomatoes Stuffed with Tuna

Prep time: 10 minutes | Cook time: 35 minutes | Serves 6

- 6 large, round, ripe firm tomatoes
- salt
- 2 seven-ounce cans imported Italian tuna packed in olive oil
- Mayonnaise, made as directed on , using the yolk of 1 large egg, ½ cup vegetable oil, and 2 tablespoons freshly squeezed lemon juice
- 2 teaspoons English or Dijon-style mustard
- 1½ tablespoons capers, soaked and rinsed if packed in salt, drained if packed in vinegar
- garnishes as suggested below

1. Prepare the tomatoes for stuffing as described in Step 1 of the recipe for Tomatoes Stuffed with Shrimp on .
2. Put the tuna in a mixing bowl and mash it to a pulp with a fork. Add the mayonnaise, holding back 1 or 2 tablespoons, the mustard, and capers. Using the fork, mix to a uniform consistency. Taste and correct for salt.
3. Shake off the excess liquid from the tomatoes without squeezing them. Stuff to the top with the tuna mixture.
4. Spread the remaining mayonnaise on top of the tomatoes, and garnish in any of the following ways: with an olive slice, a strip of red or yellow pepper, a ring of tiny capers, or 1 or 2 parsley leaves. Serve at room temperature or slightly chilled.

Roasted Branzino with Lemon

Prep time: 10 minutes | Cook time: 20 minutes | Serves 2

- 1 to 1½ pounds branzino, scaled and gutted
- Salt
- Freshly ground black pepper
- 1 tablespoon olive oil
- 1 lemon, sliced
- 3 garlic cloves, minced
- ¼ cup chopped fresh herbs (any mixture of oregano, thyme, parsley, and rosemary)

1. Preheat the oven to 425°F and set the rack to the middle position.
2. Lay the cleaned fish in a baking dish and make 4 to 5 slits in it, about 1½ inches apart.
3. Season the inside of the branzino with salt and pepper and drizzle with olive oil.
4. Fill the cavity of the fish with lemon slices. Sprinkle the chopped garlic and herbs over the lemon and close the fish.
5. Roast the fish for 15 to 20 minutes, or until the flesh is opaque and it flakes apart easily.
6. Before eating, open the fish, remove the lemon slices, and carefully pull out the bone.

Salmon with Tarragon-Dijon Sauce

Prep time: 5 minutes | Cook time: 15 minutes | Serves 4

- 1¼ pounds salmon fillet (skin on or removed), cut into 4 equal pieces
- ¼ cup avocado oil mayonnaise
- ¼ cup Dijon or stone-ground mustard
- Zest and juice of ½ lemon
- 2 tablespoons chopped fresh tarragon or 1 to 2 teaspoons dried tarragon
- ½ teaspoon salt
- ¼ teaspoon freshly ground black pepper
- 4 tablespoons extra-virgin olive oil, for serving

1. Preheat the oven to 425°F. Line a baking sheet with parchment paper.
2. Place the salmon pieces, skin-side down, on a baking sheet.
3. In a small bowl, whisk together the mayonnaise, mustard, lemon zest and juice, tarragon, salt, and pepper. Top the salmon evenly with the sauce mixture.
4. Bake until slightly browned on top and slightly translucent in the center, 10 to 12 minutes, depending on the thickness of the salmon. Remove from the oven and leave on the baking sheet for 10 minutes. Drizzle each fillet with 1 tablespoon olive oil before serving.

Air Fried Shrimp with Chili-Greek Yogurt Sauce

Prep time: 10 minutes | Cook time: 20 minutes | Serves 4

- Whole wheat bread crumbs: 3/4 cup
- Raw shrimp: 4 cups, deveined, peeled
- Flour: half cup
- Paprika: one tsp
- Chicken Seasoning, to taste
- 2 tbsp. of one egg white
- Salt and pepper to taste
- Sauce
- Sweet chili sauce: 1/4 cup
- Plain Greek yogurt: 1/3 cup
- Sriracha: 2 tbsp.

1. Let the Air Fryer preheat to 400 degrees F.
2. Add the seasonings to the shrimp and coat well.
3. In three separate bowls, add flour, bread crumbs, and egg whites.
4. First coat the shrimp in flour, dab lightly in egg whites, then in the bread crumbs.
5. with cook oil, spray the shrimp. Place the shrimp in an Air Fryer, cook for four minutes, turn the shrimp over, and cook for another four minutes. Serve with sauce.

Sauce:
1. Mix all the ingredients.

Catfish with Green Beans

Prep time: 10 minutes | Cook time: 20 minutes | Serves 2

- Catfish fillets: 2 pieces
- Green beans: half cup, trimmed
- Honey: 2 teaspoon
- Ground black pepper and salt, to taste divided
- Crushed red pepper: half tsp.
- Flour: 1/4 cup
- One egg, lightly beaten
- Dill pickle relish: 3/4 teaspoon
- Apple cider vinegar: half tsp
- 1/3 cup whole-wheat breadcrumbs
- Mayonnaise: 2 tablespoons
- Dill
- Lemon wedges

1. In a bowl, add green beans and spray them with cook oil. Coat with crushed red pepper, 1/8 teaspoon of salt, and half tsp. of honey. Cook in the Air Fryer at 400°F until soft and browned, for 12 minutes
2. Take out from the Air Fryer and cover with aluminum foil.
3. In the meantime, coat catfish in flour. Then coat in egg, then in breadcrumbs. Place the catfish in an Air Fryer basket and spray with cook oil. Cook for 8 minutes at 400°F, until golden brown.
4. Sprinkle with pepper and salt.
5. In the meantime, mix vinegar, dill, relish, mayonnaise, and honey in a bowl. Serve the sauce with fish and green beans.

Chapter 9

Vegetables and Vegan

Vegetable Paella

Prep time: 10 minutes | Cook time 85 minutes | Serves 6

- 3 cups jarred whole baby artichokes packed in water, quartered, rinsed, and patted dry
- 2 red bell peppers, stemmed, seeded, and chopped coarse
- ½ cup pitted kalamata olives, chopped
- 9 garlic cloves, peeled (3 whole, 6 minced)
- 6 tablespoons extra-virgin olive oil
- Salt and pepper
- 3 tablespoons chopped fresh parsley
- 2 tablespoons lemon juice
- 1 onion, chopped fine
- 1 fennel bulb, stalks discarded, bulb halved, cored, and sliced thin
- ½ teaspoon smoked paprika
- 1 (14.5-ounce) can diced tomatoes, drained, minced, and drained again
- 2 cups Bomba rice
- 3 cups vegetable broth
- ⅓ cup dry white wine
- ½ teaspoon saffron threads, crumbled
- ½ cup frozen peas, thawed

1. Adjust oven rack to lower-middle position, place rimmed baking sheet on rack, and heat oven to 450 degrees. Toss artichokes and peppers with olives, whole garlic cloves, 2 tablespoons oil, ½ teaspoon salt, and ¼ teaspoon pepper in bowl. Spread vegetables in hot sheet and roast until artichokes are browned around edges and peppers are browned, 20 to 25 minutes; let cool slightly.
2. Mince roasted garlic. In large bowl, whisk 2 tablespoons oil, 2 tablespoons parsley, lemon juice, and minced roasted garlic together. Add roasted vegetables and toss to combine. Season with salt and pepper to taste.
3. Reduce oven temperature to 350 degrees. Heat remaining 2 tablespoons oil in Dutch oven over medium heat until shimmering. Add onion and fennel and cook until softened, 8 to 10 minutes.
4. For optional socarrat, transfer pot to stovetop and remove lid. Cook over medium-high heat for about 5 minutes, rotating pot as needed, until bottom layer of rice is well browned and crisp.
5. Sprinkle roasted vegetables and peas over rice, cover, and let paella sit for 5 minutes. Sprinkle with remaining 1 tablespoon parsley and serve.

Herbed Ricotta-Stuffed Mushrooms

Prep time: 10 minutes | Cook time:30 minutes |Serves 4

- 6 tablespoons extra-virgin olive oil, divided
- 4 portobello mushroom caps, cleaned and gills removed
- 1 cup whole-milk ricotta cheese
- 2 garlic cloves, finely minced
- ½ teaspoon salt
- ¼ teaspoon freshly ground black pepper

1. Preheat the oven to 400°F.
2. Line a baking sheet with parchment or foil and drizzle with 2 tablespoons olive oil, spreading evenly. Place the mushroom caps on the baking sheet, gill-side up.
3. In a medium bowl, mix together the ricotta, herbs, 2 tablespoons olive oil, garlic, salt, and pepper. Stuff each mushroom cap with one-quarter of the cheese mixture, pressing down if needed.
4. Drizzle with remaining 2 tablespoons olive oil and bake until golden brown and the mushrooms are soft, 30 to 35 minutes, depending on the size of the mushrooms.

The Mediterranean Diet Cookbook for Beginners

Moroccan Vegetable Tagine

Prep time: 20 minutes | **Cook time:** 1 hour | **Serves 6**

- ½ cup extra-virgin olive oil
- 2 medium yellow onions, sliced
- 6 celery stalks, sliced into ¼-inch crescents
- 6 garlic cloves, minced
- 1 teaspoon ground cumin
- 1 teaspoon ginger powder
- 1 teaspoon salt
- ½ teaspoon paprika
- ½ teaspoon ground cinnamon
- ¼ teaspoon freshly ground black pepper
- 2 cups vegetable stock
- 1 medium eggplant, cut into 1-inch cubes
- 2 medium zucchini, cut into ½-inch-thick semicircles
- 2 cups cauliflower florets
- 1 (13.75-ounce) can artichoke hearts, drained and quartered
- 1 cup halved and pitted green olives
- ½ cup chopped fresh flat-leaf parsley, for garnish
- ½ cup chopped fresh cilantro leaves, for garnish
- Greek yogurt, for garnish (optional)

1. In a large, thick soup pot or Dutch oven, heat the olive oil over medium-high heat. Add the onion and celery and sauté until softened, 6 to 8 minutes. Add the garlic, cumin, ginger, salt, paprika, cinnamon, and pepper and sauté for another 2 minutes.
2. Add the stock and bring to a boil. Reduce the heat to low and add the eggplant, zucchini, and cauliflower. Simmer on low heat, covered, until the vegetables are tender, 30 to 35 minutes. Add the artichoke hearts and olives, cover, and simmer for another 15 minutes.
3. Serve garnished with parsley, cilantro, and Greek yogurt (if using).

Braised Carrots with Capers

Prep time: 10 minutes | **Cook time:** 25 minutes | **Serves 4**

- 1 pound choice young carrots
- 3 tablespoons extra virgin olive oil
- 1 teaspoon chopped garlic
- 2 tablespoons chopped parsley
- black pepper, ground fresh from the mill
- 2 tablespoons capers, soaked and rinsed if packed in salt, drained if in vinegar
- salt

1. Peel the carrots and wash them in cold water. They ought to be no thicker than your little finger. If they are not that size to start with, cut them lengthwise in half, or in quarters if necessary.
2. Choose a sauté pan that can later accommodate all the carrots loosely. Put in the olive oil and garlic, and turn on the heat to medium high. Cook and stir the garlic until it becomes colored a pale gold, then add the carrots and parsley. Toss the carrots once or twice to coat them well, then add ¼ cup water. When the water has completely evaporated, add another ¼ cup. Continue adding water at this pace, whenever it has evaporated, until the carrots are done. They should feel tender, but firm, when prodded with a fork. Test them from time to time. Depending on the youth and freshness of the carrots, it should take about 20 to 30 minutes. When done, there should be no more water left in the pan. If there is still some, boil it away quickly, and let the carrots brown lightly.
3. Add pepper and the capers, and toss the carrots once or twice. Cook for another minute or two, then taste and correct for salt, stir once again, transfer to a warm platter, and serve at once.

Walnut Pesto Zoodles

Prep time: 15 minutes | Cook time: 10 minutes| Serves 4

- 4 medium zucchini (makes about 8 cups of zoodles)
- ¼ cup extra-virgin olive oil, divided
- 2 garlic cloves, minced (about 1 teaspoon), divided
- ½ teaspoon crushed red pepper
- ¼ teaspoon freshly ground black pepper, divided
- ¼ teaspoon kosher or sea salt, divided
- 2 tablespoons grated Parmesan cheese, divided
- 1 cup packed fresh basil leaves
- ¾ cup walnut pieces, divided

1. Make the zucchini noodles (zoodles) using a spiralizer or your vegetable peeler to make ribbons (run the peeler down the zucchini to make long strips). In a large bowl, gently mix to combine the zoodles with 1 tablespoon of oil, 1 minced garlic clove, all the crushed red pepper, ⅛ teaspoon of black pepper, and ⅛ teaspoon of salt. Set aside.
2. In a large skillet over medium-high heat, heat ½ tablespoon of oil. Add half of the zoodles to the pan and cook for 5 minutes, stirring every minute or so. Pour the cooked zoodles into a large serving bowl, and repeat with another ½ tablespoon of oil and the remaining zoodles. Add those zoodles to the serving bowl when they are done cooking.
3. While the zoodles are cooking, make the pesto. If you're using a food processor, add the remaining minced garlic clove, ⅛ teaspoon of black pepper, and ⅛ teaspoon of salt, 1 tablespoon of Parmesan, all the basil leaves, and ¼ cup of walnuts. Turn on the processor, and slowly drizzle the remaining 2 tablespoons of oil into the opening until the pesto is completely blended. If you're using a high-powered blender, add the 2 tablespoons of oil first and then the rest of the pesto ingredients. Pulse until the pesto is completely blended.
4. Add the pesto to the zoodles along with the remaining 1 tablespoon of Parmesan and the remaining ½ cup of walnuts. Mix together well and serve.

Stuffed Cucumber Cups

Prep time: 5 minutes| Cook time: 15 minutes | Serves 2

- 1 medium cucumber (about 8 ounces, 8 to 9 inches long)
- ½ cup hummus (any flavor) or white bean dip
- 4 or 5 cherry tomatoes, sliced in half
- 2 tablespoons fresh basil, minced

1. Slice the ends off the cucumber (about ½ inch from each side) and slice the cucumber into 1-inch pieces.
2. with a paring knife or a spoon, scoop most of the seeds from the inside of each cucumber piece to make a cup, being careful to not cut all the way through.
3. Fill each cucumber cup with about 1 tablespoon of hummus or bean dip.
4. Top each with a cherry tomato half and a sprinkle of fresh minced basil.

Orange-Glazed Carrots

Prep time: 10 minutes | Cook time: 4 to 6 hours | Serves 8

- 3 pounds carrots, peeled and cut into ¼-inch slices on the bias
- 1½ cups water, plus extra hot water as needed
- 1 tablespoon granulated sugar
- 1 teaspoon sea salt
- ½ Cup orange marmalade
- 2 tablespoons unsalted butter, softened
- 1½ teaspoons fresh sage, minced
- Black pepper (optional)

1. Combine the carrots, 1½ cups water, sugar, and 1 teaspoon salt in the slow cooker. Cover and cook on low until the carrots are tender, 4 to 6 hours.
2. Drain the carrots, and then return to the slow cooker. Stir in the marmalade, butter, and sage. Season with additional salt and some pepper, if needed. Serve hot. (If needed, you may keep this dish on the warm setting for 1 to 2 hours before serving. Stir in some hot water before serving if it gets too thick.)

Bite-Size Stuffed Peppers

Prep time: 15 minutes | Cook time: 10 minutes | Serves 8-10

- 20 to 25 mini sweet bell peppers, assortment of colors
- 1 tablespoon extra-virgin olive oil
- 4 ounces goat cheese, at room temperature
- 4 ounces mascarpone cheese, at room temperature
- 1 tablespoon fresh chives, chopped
- 1 tablespoon lemon zest

1. Preheat the oven to 400°F.
2. Remove the stem, cap, and any seeds from the peppers. Put them into a bowl and toss to coat with the olive oil.
3. Put the peppers onto a baking sheet | bake for 8 minutes.
4. Remove the peppers from the oven and let cool completely.
5. In a medium bowl, add the goat cheese, mascarpone cheese, chives, and lemon zest. Stir to combine, then spoon mixture into a piping bag.
6. Fill each pepper to the top with the cheese mixture, using the piping bag.
7. Chill the peppers in the fridge for at least 30 minutes before serving.

Lemon-Rosemary Beets

Prep time: 10 minutes | Cook time: 8 hours | Serves 7

- 2 pounds beets, peeled and cut into wedges
- 2 tablespoons fresh lemon juice
- 2 tablespoons extra-virgin olive oil
- 2 tablespoons honey
- 1 tablespoon apple cider vinegar
- ¾ teaspoon sea salt
- ½ teaspoon black pepper
- 2 sprigs fresh rosemary
- ½ Teaspoon lemon zest

1. Place the beets in the slow cooker.
2. Whisk the lemon juice, extra-virgin olive oil, honey, apple cider vinegar, salt, and pepper together in a small bowl. Pour over the beets.
3. Add the sprigs of rosemary to the slow cooker.
4. Cover and cook on low for 8 hours, or until the beets are tender.
5. Remove and discard the rosemary sprigs. Stir in the lemon zest. Serve hot.

Linguine and Brussels Sprouts

Prep time: 10 minutes | Cook time: 25 minutes | Serves 4

- 8 ounces whole-wheat linguine
- ⅓ cup, plus 2 tablespoons extra-virgin olive oil, divided
- 1 medium sweet onion, diced
- 2 to 3 garlic cloves, smashed
- 8 ounces Brussels sprouts, chopped
- ½ cup chicken stock, as needed
- ⅓ cup dry white wine
- ½ cup shredded Parmesan cheese
- 1 lemon, cut in quarters

1. Bring a large pot of water to a boil and cook the pasta according to package directions. Drain, reserving 1 cup of the pasta water. Mix the cooked pasta with 2 tablespoons of olive oil, then set aside.
2. In a large sauté pan or skillet, heat the remaining ⅓ cup of olive oil on medium heat. Add the onion to the pan and cook for about 5 minutes, until softened. Add the smashed garlic cloves and cook for 1 minute, until fragrant.
3. Add the Brussels sprouts and cook covered for 15 minutes. Add chicken stock as needed to prevent burning. Once Brussels sprouts have wilted and are fork-tender, add white wine and cook down for about 7 minutes, until reduced.
4. Add the pasta to the skillet and add the pasta water as needed.
5. Serve with the Parmesan cheese and lemon for squeezing over the dish right before eating.

Spicy Roasted Potatoes

Prep time: 20 minutes | Cook time: 25 minutes | Serves 5

- 1½ pounds red potatoes or gold potatoes
- 3 tablespoons garlic, minced
- 1½ teaspoons salt
- ¼ cup extra-virgin olive oil
- ½ cup fresh cilantro, chopped
- ½ teaspoon freshly ground black pepper
- ¼ teaspoon cayenne pepper
- 3 tablespoons lemon juice

1. Preheat the oven to 450°F.
2. Scrub the potatoes and pat dry.
3. Cut the potatoes into ½-inch pieces and put them into a bowl.
4. Add the garlic, salt, and olive oil and toss everything together to evenly coat.
5. Pour the potato mixture onto a baking sheet, spread the potatoes out evenly, and put them into the oven, roasting for 25 minutes. Halfway through roasting, turn the potatoes with a spatula | continue roasting for the remainder of time until the potato edges start to brown.
6. Remove the potatoes from the oven and let them cool on the baking sheet for 5 minutes.
7. Using a spatula, remove the potatoes from the pan and put them into a bowl.
8. Add the cilantro, black pepper, cayenne, and lemon juice to the potatoes and toss until well mixed. Serve warm.

Cauliflower Steaks with Eggplant Relish

Prep time: 5 minutes | Cook time: 25 minutes | Serves 4

- 2 small heads cauliflower (about 3 pounds)
- ¼ teaspoon kosher or sea salt
- ¼ teaspoon smoked paprika
- extra-virgin olive oil, divided
- 1 recipe Eggplant Relish Spread or 1 container store-bought baba ghanoush

1. Place a large, rimmed baking sheet in the oven. Preheat the oven to 400°F with the pan inside.
2. Stand one head of cauliflower on a cutting board, stem-end down. with a long chef's knife, slice down through the very center of the head, including the stem. Starting at the cut edge, measure about 1 inch and cut one thick slice from each cauliflower half, including as much of the stem as possible, to make two cauliflower "steaks." Reserve the remaining cauliflower for another use. Repeat with the second cauliflower head.
3. Dry each steak well with a clean towel. Sprinkle the salt and smoked paprika evenly over both sides of each cauliflower steak.
4. Using oven mitts, carefully remove the baking sheet from the oven and place the cauliflower on the baking sheet. Roast in the oven for 12 to 15 minutes, until the cauliflower steaks are just fork tender; they will still be somewhat firm. Serve the steaks with the Eggplant Relish Spread, baba ghanoush, or the homemade ketchup from our Italian Baked Beans recipe.

Fresh Veggie Frittata

Prep time: 5 minutes | Cook time: 15 minutes | Serves 1

- 3 large eggs
- 1 teaspoon almond milk
- 1 tablespoon olive oil
- 1 handful baby spinach leaves
- 1/2 baby eggplant, peeled and diced
- 1/4 small red bell pepper, chopped
- Sea salt and freshly ground pepper, to taste
- 1 ounce crumbled goat cheese

1. Preheat the broiler.
2. Beat the eggs with the almond milk until just combined.
3. Heat a small nonstick, broiler-proof skillet over medium-high heat. Add the olive oil, followed by the eggs.
4. Spread the spinach on top of the egg mixture in an even layer and top with the rest of the veggies.
5. Reduce heat to medium and season with sea salt and freshly ground pepper to taste. Allow the eggs and vegetables to cook 3–5 minutes until the bottom half of the eggs are firm and vegetables are tender.
6. Top with the crumbled goat cheese and place on middle rack under the broiler, and then cook another 3–5 minutes until the eggs are firm in the middle and the cheese has melted.
7. Slice into wedges and serve immediately.

The Mediterranean Diet Cookbook for Beginners

Smothered Cabbage

Prep time: 10 minutes | Cook time: 35 minutes | Serves 6

- 2 pounds green, red, or savoy cabbage
- ½ cup chopped onion
- ½ cup extra virgin olive oil
- 1 tablespoon chopped garlic
- salt
- black pepper, ground fresh from the mill
- 1 tablespoon wine vinegar

1. Detach and discard the first few outer leaves of the cabbage. The remaining head of leaves must be shredded very fine. If you are going to do it by hand, cut the leaves into fine shreds, slicing them off the whole head. Turn the head after you have sliced a section of it until gradually you expose the entire core, which must be discarded. If you want to use the food processor, cut the leaves off from the core in sections, discard the core, and process the leaves through a shredding attachment.
2. Put the onion and olive oil into a large sauté pan, and turn the heat on to medium. Cook and stir the onion until it becomes colored a deep gold, then add the garlic. When you have cooked the garlic until it becomes colored a very pale gold, add the shredded cabbage. Turn the cabbage over 2 or 3 times to coat it well, and cook it until it is wilted.
3. Add salt, pepper, and the vinegar. Turn the cabbage over once completely, lower the heat to minimum, and cover the pan tightly. Cook for at least 1½ hours, or until it is very tender, turning it from time to time. If while it is cooking, the liquid in the pan should become insufficient, add 2 tablespoons water as needed. When done, taste and correct for salt and pepper. Allow it to settle a few minutes off heat before serving.

Citrus Asparagus with Pistachios

Prep time: 10 minutes | Cook time: 15 minutes | Serves 4

- 5 tablespoons extra-virgin olive oil, divided
- Zest and juice of 2 clementines or 1 orange (about ¼ cup juice and 1 tablespoon zest)
- Zest and juice of 1 lemon
- 1 tablespoon red wine vinegar
- 1 teaspoon salt, divided
- ¼ teaspoon freshly ground black pepper
- ½ cup shelled pistachios
- 1 pound fresh asparagus
- 1 tablespoon water

1. In a small bowl, whisk together 4 tablespoons olive oil, the clementine and lemon juices and zests, vinegar, ½ teaspoon salt, and pepper. Set aside.
2. In a medium dry skillet, toast the pistachios over medium-high heat until lightly browned, 2 to 3 minutes, being careful not to let them burn. Transfer to a cutting board and coarsely chop. Set aside.
3. Trim the rough ends off the asparagus, usually the last 1 to 2 inches of each spear. In a skillet, heat the remaining 1 tablespoon olive oil over medium-high heat. Add the asparagus and sauté for 2 to 3 minutes. Sprinkle with the remaining ½ teaspoon salt and add the water. Reduce the heat to medium-low, cover, and cook until tender, another 2 to 4 minutes, depending on the thickness of the spears.
4. Transfer the cooked asparagus to a serving dish. Add the pistachios to the dressing and whisk to combine. Pour the dressing over the warm asparagus and toss to coat.

Chapter 10

Desserts

Nut Butter Cup Fat Bomb

Prep time: 5 minutes | Cook time: 5 minutes | Serves 8

- ½ cup crunchy almond butter (no sugar added)
- ½ cup light fruity extra-virgin olive oil
- ¼ cup ground flaxseed
- 2 tablespoons unsweetened cocoa powder
- 1 teaspoon vanilla extract
- 1 teaspoon ground cinnamon (optional)
- 1 to 2 teaspoons sugar-free sweetener of choice (optional)

1. In a mixing bowl, combine the almond butter, olive oil, flaxseed, cocoa powder, vanilla, cinnamon (if using), and sweetener (if using) and stir well with a spatula to combine. Mixture will be a thick liquid.
2. Pour into 8 mini muffin liners and freeze until solid, at least 12 hours. Store in the freezer to maintain their shape.

Homemade Sea Salt Pita Chips

Prep time: 2 minutes | Cook time: 8 minutes | Serves 2

- 2 whole wheat pitas
- 1 tablespoon olive oil
- ½ teaspoon kosher salt

1. Preheat the air fryer to 360°F.
2. Cut each pita into 8 wedges.
3. In a medium bowl, toss the pita wedges, olive oil, and salt until the wedges are coated and the olive oil and salt are evenly distributed.
4. Place the pita wedges into the air fryer basket in an even layer and fry for 6 to 8 minutes. (The cooking time will vary depending upon how thick the pita is and how browned you prefer a chip.)
5. Season with additional salt, if desired. Serve alone or with a favorite dip.

Dark Chocolate Lava Cake

Prep time: 5 minutes | Cook time: 10 minutes | Serves 4

- Olive oil cooking spray
- ¼ cup whole wheat flour
- 1 tablespoon unsweetened dark chocolate cocoa powder
- ⅛ teaspoon salt
- ½ teaspoon baking powder
- ¼ cup raw honey
- 1 egg
- 2 tablespoons olive oil

1. Preheat the air fryer to 380°F. Lightly coat the insides of four ramekins with olive oil cooking spray.
2. In a medium bowl, combine the flour, cocoa powder, salt, baking powder, honey, egg, and olive oil.
3. Divide the batter evenly among the ramekins.
4. Place the filled ramekins inside the air fryer and bake for 10 minutes.
5. Remove the lava cakes from the air fryer and slide a knife around the outside edge of each cake. Turn each ramekin upside down on a saucer and serve.

Baked Spanakopita Dip

Prep time: 10 minutes | Cook time: 15 minutes | Serves 2

- Olive oil cooking spray
- 3 tablespoons olive oil, divided
- 2 tablespoons minced white onion
- 2 garlic cloves, minced
- 4 cups fresh spinach
- 4 ounces cream cheese, softened
- 4 ounces feta cheese, divided
- Zest of 1 lemon
- ¼ teaspoon ground nutmeg
- 1 teaspoon dried dill
- ½ teaspoon salt
- Pita chips, carrot sticks, or sliced bread for serving (optional)

1. Preheat the air fryer to 360°F. Coat the inside of a 6-inch ramekin or baking dish with olive oil cooking spray.
2. In a large skillet over medium heat, heat 1 tablespoon of the olive oil. Add the onion, then cook for 1 minute.
3. Add in the garlic and cook, stirring for 1 minute more.
4. Reduce the heat to low and mix in the spinach and water. Let this cook for 2 to 3 minutes, or until the spinach has wilted. Remove the skillet from the heat.
5. In a medium bowl, combine the cream cheese, 2 ounces of the feta, and the remaining 2 tablespoons of olive oil, along with the lemon zest, nutmeg, dill, and salt. Mix until just combined.
6. Add the vegetables to the cheese base and stir until combined.
7. Pour the dip mixture into the prepared ramekin and top with the remaining 2 ounces of feta cheese.
8. Place the dip into the air fryer basket and cook for 10 minutes, or until heated through and bubbling.
9. Serve with pita chips, carrot sticks, or sliced bread.

Apple Chips with Chocolate Tahini

Prep time: 10 minutes | Cook time: 15 minutes | Serves 2

- 2 tablespoons tahini
- 1 tablespoon maple syrup
- 1 tablespoon unsweetened cocoa powder
- 1 to 2 tablespoons warm water (or more if needed)
- 2 medium apples
- 1 tablespoon roasted, salted sunflower seeds

1. In a small bowl, mix together the tahini, maple syrup, and cocoa powder. Add warm water, a little at a time, until thin enough to drizzle. Do not microwave it to thin it—it won't work.
2. Slice the apples crosswise into round slices, and then cut each piece in half to make a chip.
3. Lay the apple chips out on a plate and drizzle them with the chocolate tahini sauce.
4. Sprinkle sunflower seeds over the apple chips.

Pumpkin-Ricotta Cheesecake

Prep time: 25 minutes | Cook time: 45 minutes | Serves 10 to 12

- 1 cup almond flour
- ½ cup butter, melted
- 1 (14.5-ounce) can pumpkin purée
- 8 ounces cream cheese, at room temperature
- ½ cup whole-milk ricotta cheese
- ½ to ¾ cup sugar-free sweetener
- 4 large eggs
- 2 teaspoons vanilla extract
- 2 teaspoons pumpkin pie spice
- Whipped cream, for garnish (optional)

1. Preheat the oven to 350°F. Line the bottom of a 9-inch springform pan with parchment paper.
2. In a small bowl, combine the almond flour and melted butter with a fork until well combined. Using your fingers, press the mixture into the bottom of the prepared pan.
3. In a large bowl, beat together the pumpkin purée, cream cheese, ricotta, and sweetener using an electric mixer on medium.
4. Pour the mixture over the crust and bake until set, 40 to 45 minutes.
5. Allow to cool to room temperature. Refrigerate for at least 6 hours before serving.
6. Serve chilled, garnishing with whipped cream, if desired.

Spiced Biscotti

Prep time: 5 minutes | Cook time 60 minutes | Serves 4

- 2¼ cups (11¼ ounces) all-purpose flour
- 1 teaspoon baking powder
- ½ teaspoon baking soda
- ½ teaspoon ground cloves
- ½ teaspoon ground cinnamon
- ¼ teaspoon ground ginger
- ¼ teaspoon salt
- ¼ teaspoon ground white pepper
- 1 cup (7 ounces) sugar
- ½ teaspoon vanilla extract

1. Adjust oven rack to middle position and heat oven to 350 degrees. Using ruler and pencil, draw two 13 by 2-inch rectangles, spaced 3 inches apart, on piece of parchment paper. Grease baking sheet and place parchment on it, marked side down.
2. Whisk flour, baking powder, baking soda, cloves, cinnamon, ginger, salt, and pepper together in small bowl. In large bowl, whisk sugar and eggs and egg yolks together until pale yellow. Whisk in vanilla until combined. Using rubber spatula, stir in flour mixture until just combined.
3. Divide dough in half. Using floured hands, form each half into 13 by 2-inch rectangle, using lines on parchment as guide. Using rubber spatula lightly coated with vegetable oil spray, smooth tops and sides of loaves. Bake until loaves are golden and just beginning to crack on top, about 35 minutes, rotating sheet halfway through baking.
4. Let loaves cool on sheet for 10 minutes, then transfer to cutting board. Reduce oven temperature to 325 degrees. Using serrated knife, slice each loaf on slight bias into ½-inch-thick slices.
5. Arrange cookies cut side down on sheet about ½ inch apart and bake until crisp and golden brown on both sides, about 15 minutes, flipping cookies halfway through baking. Let cool completely on wire rack before serving. (Biscotti can be stored at room temperature for up to 1 month.)

Red Pepper Coques

Prep time: 10 minutes | Cook time 65 minutes | Serves 6-8

Dough
- 3 cups (16½ ounces) bread flour
- 2 teaspoons sugar
- ½ teaspoon instant or rapid-rise yeast
- 1⅓ cups ice water
- 3 tablespoons extra-virgin olive oil
- 1½ teaspoons salt

Topping
- ½ cup extra-virgin olive oil
- 2 large onions, halved and sliced thin
- 2 cups jarred roasted red peppers, patted dry and sliced thin
- 3 tablespoons sugar
- 3 garlic cloves, minced
- 1½ teaspoons salt
- ¼ teaspoon red pepper flakes
- 3 tablespoons sherry vinegar
- ¼ cup pine nuts (optional)
- 1 tablespoon minced fresh parsley

For the dough
1. Pulse flour, sugar, and yeast in food processor until combined, about 5 pulses. with processor running, slowly add ice water and process until dough is just combined and no dry flour remains, about 10 seconds. Let dough rest for 10 minutes.
2. Add oil and salt to dough and process until dough forms satiny, sticky ball that clears sides of bowl, 30 to 60 seconds. Transfer dough to lightly floured counter and knead by hand to form smooth, round ball, about 30 seconds. Place dough seam side down in lightly greased large bowl or container, cover tightly with plastic wrap, and refrigerate for at least 24 hours or up to 3 days.

For the topping
1. Heat 3 tablespoons oil in 12-inch nonstick skillet over medium heat until shimmering. Stir in onions, red peppers, sugar, garlic, salt, pepper flakes, and bay leaves. Cover and cook, stirring occasionally, until onions are softened and have released their juice, about 10 minutes. Remove lid and continue to cook, stirring often, until onions are golden brown, 10 to 15 minutes. Off heat, discard bay leaves. Transfer onion mixture to bowl, stir in vinegar, and let cool completely before using.
2. Press down on dough to deflate. Transfer dough to clean counter, divide into quarters, and cover loosely with greased plastic. Working with 1 piece of dough at a time (keep remaining pieces covered), form into rough ball by stretching dough around your thumbs and pinching edges together so that top is smooth.
3. Place ball seam side down on counter and, using your cupped hands, drag in small circles until dough feels taut and round. Space dough balls 3 inches apart, cover loosely with greased plastic, and let rest for 1 hour.
4. Brush dough ovals with remaining 1 tablespoon oil and bake until puffed, 6 to 8 minutes, switching and rotating sheets halfway through baking.
5. Scatter onion mixture evenly over flatbreads, from edge to edge, then sprinkle with pine nuts, if using. Bake until topping is heated through and edges of flatbreads are deep golden brown and crisp, about 15 minutes, switching and rotating sheets halfway through baking. Let flatbreads cool on sheets for 10 minutes, then transfer to cutting board using metal spatula. Sprinkle with parsley, slice, and serve.

Strawberry Caprese Skewers

Prep time: 15 minutes | Cook time: 15 minutes | Serves 2

- ½ cup balsamic vinegar
- 16 whole, hulled strawberries
- 12 small basil leaves or 6 large leaves, halved
- 12 pieces of small mozzarella balls (ciliegine)

1. To make the balsamic glaze, pour the balsamic vinegar into a small saucepan and bring it to a boil. Reduce the heat to medium-low and simmer for 10 minutes, or until it's reduced by half and is thick enough to coat the back of a spoon.
2. On each of 4 wooden skewers, place a strawberry, a folded basil leaf, and a mozzarella ball, repeating twice and adding a strawberry on the end. (Each skewer should have 4 strawberries, 3 basil leaves, and 3 mozzarella balls.)
3. Drizzle 1 to 2 teaspoons of balsamic glaze over the skewers.

Baked Apples with Amaretti Cookies

Prep time: 10 minutes | Cook time: 25 minutes | Serves 4

- 4 crisp, tart-sweet apples
- 9 pairs imported Italian amaretti cookies
- 4 tablespoons (½ stick) butter, completely softened at room temperature
- ¼ cup granulated sugar
- ½ cup water mixed with ½ cup dry white wine

1. Preheat oven to 400°.
2. Wash the apples in cold water. Use any suitable tool, from an apple corer to a pointed vegetable peeler, to core them from the top, stopping short of the bottom. Create a hole in the center that is ½ inch broad. Prick the apples' skin in many places, every inch or so, using a pointed knife blade.
3. Double a sheet of wax paper around 7 pairs of the amaretti, and pound them with a heavy object, such as a mallet or meat pounder, until they are crushed to a coarse consistency, but not pulverized. Mix them thoroughly with the very soft butter. Divide the mixture into 4 parts, and pack one part tightly into each apple cavity.
4. Put the apples in a baking pan, right side up. Sprinkle a tablespoon of sugar over each, and pour over them the water and white wine. Place the pan on the uppermost rack of the preheated oven and bake for 45 minutes.
5. There will be some liquid left in the baking pan. Separate the remaining 2 pairs of amaretti, and dip each cookie in the pan, but do not let it become too soggy or it will crumble. Put one of the cookies over the opening of each apple.
6. If the baking pan cannot go over direct heat, pour its contents into a saucepan, and turn the heat on to high. When the liquid has cooked down to a syrupy consistency, pour it over the apples. Serve at room temperature.

Lemon-Anise Biscotti

Prep time 5 minutes | Cook time: 50 minutes | Serves 4

- 2 cups (10 ounces) all-purpose flour
- 1 teaspoon baking powder
- ¼ teaspoon salt
- 1 cup (7 ounces) sugar
- 2 large eggs
- 1 tablespoon grated lemon zest
- 1 tablespoon anise seeds
- ¼ teaspoon vanilla extract

1. Adjust oven rack to middle position and heat oven to 350 degrees. Using ruler and pencil, draw two 13 by 2-inch rectangles, spaced 3 inches apart, on piece of parchment paper. Grease baking sheet and place parchment on it, marked side down.
2. Whisk flour, baking powder, and salt together in small bowl. In large bowl, whisk sugar and eggs together until pale yellow. Whisk in lemon zest, anise seeds, and vanilla until combined. Using rubber spatula, stir in flour mixture until just combined.
3. Divide dough in half. Using floured hands, form each half into 13 by 2-inch rectangle, using lines on parchment as guide. Using rubber spatula lightly coated with vegetable oil spray, smooth tops and sides of loaves. Bake until loaves are golden and just beginning to crack on top, about 35 minutes, rotating sheet halfway through baking.
4. Let loaves cool on sheet for 10 minutes, then transfer to cutting board. Reduce oven temperature to 325 degrees. Using serrated knife, slice each loaf on slight bias into ½-inch-thick slices.
5. Arrange cookies cut side down on sheet about ½ inch apart and bake until crisp and golden brown on both sides, about 15 minutes, flipping cookies halfway through baking. Let cool completely on wire rack before serving. (Biscotti can be stored at room temperature for up to 1 month.)

Chocolate Pudding

Prep time: 10 minutes | Cook time: 5 minutes | Serves 4

- 2 ripe avocados, halved and pitted
- ¼ cup unsweetened cocoa powder
- ¼ cup heavy whipping cream, plus more if needed
- 2 teaspoons vanilla extract
- ½ teaspoon ground cinnamon (optional)
- ¼ teaspoon salt
- Whipped cream, for serving (optional)

1. Using a spoon, scoop out the ripe avocado into a blender or large bowl, if using an immersion blender. Mash well with a fork.
2. Add the cocoa powder, heavy whipping cream, vanilla, sweetener (if using), cinnamon (if using), and salt. Blend well until smooth and creamy, adding additional cream, 1 tablespoon at a time, if the mixture is too thick.
3. Cover and refrigerate for at least 1 hour before serving. Serve chilled with additional whipped cream, if desired.

Manchego Crackers

Prep time: 15 minutes | Cook time: 15 minutes | Serves 4

- 4 tablespoons butter, at room temperature
- 1 cup finely shredded Manchego cheese
- 1 cup almond flour
- 1 teaspoon salt, divided
- ¼ teaspoon freshly ground black pepper
- 1 large egg

1. Using an electric mixer, cream together the butter and shredded cheese until well combined and smooth.
2. In a small bowl, combine the almond flour with ½ teaspoon salt and pepper. Slowly add the almond flour mixture to the cheese, mixing constantly until the dough just comes together to form a ball.
3. Transfer to a piece of parchment or plastic wrap and roll into a cylinder log about 1½ inches thick. Wrap tightly and refrigerate for at least 1 hour.
4. Preheat the oven to 350°F. Line two baking sheets with parchment paper or silicone baking mats.
5. Slice the refrigerated dough into small rounds, about ¼ inch thick, and place on the lined baking sheets.
6. Brush the tops of the crackers with egg wash and bake until the crackers are golden and crispy, 12 to 15 minutes. Remove from the oven and allow to cool on a wire rack.
7. Serve warm or, once fully cooled, store in an airtight container in the refrigerator for up to 1 week.

Zesty Green Bites

Prep time: 5 minutes | Cook time: 45 minutes | Serves 8

- ¼ cup frozen chopped kale
- ¼ cup finely chopped artichoke hearts
- ¼ cup ricotta cheese
- 2 tbsp grated Parmesan cheese
- ¼ cup goat cheese
- 1 large egg white
- 1 tsp dried basil
- 1 lemon, zested
- ½ tsp salt
- ½ tsp freshly ground black pepper
- 4 frozen filo dough, thawed
- 1 tbsp extra-virgin olive oil

1. In a bowl, combine kale, artichoke, ricotta, parmesan, goat cheese, egg white, basil, lemon zest, salt, and pepper. Place a filo dough on a clean flat surface. Brush with olive oil.
2. Place a second filo sheet on the first and brush with more oil. Continue layering to form a pile of four oiled sheets. Working from the short side, cut the phyllo sheets into 8 strips and half them.
3. Spoon 1 tablespoon of filling onto one short end of every strip. Fold a corner to cover the filling and a triangle; continue folding over and over to the end of the strip, creating a triangle-shaped filo packet.
4. Repeat the process with the other filo bites. Place a trivet into the pot. Pour in 1 cup of water. Place the bites on top of the trivet. Seal the lid and cook on High Pressure for 15 minutes. Do a quick release.

Burrata Caprese Stack

Prep time: 5 minutes | Cook time: 5 minutes | Serves 4

- 1 large organic tomato, preferably heirloom
- ½ teaspoon salt
- ¼ teaspoon freshly ground black pepper
- 1 (4-ounce) ball burrata cheese
- 8 fresh basil leaves, thinly sliced
- 2 tablespoons extra-virgin olive oil
- 1 tablespoon red wine or balsamic vinegar

1. Slice the tomato into 4 thick slices, removing any tough center core and sprinkle with salt and pepper. Place the tomatoes, seasoned-side up, on a plate.
2. On a separate rimmed plate, slice the burrata into 4 thick slices and place one slice on top of each tomato slice. Top each with one-quarter of the basil and pour any reserved burrata cream from the rimmed plate over top.
3. Drizzle with olive oil and vinegar and serve with a fork and knife.

Honey-Lavender Biscotti

Prep time: 5 minutes | Cook time 60 minutes | Serves 4

- 2¼ cups (11¼ ounces) all-purpose flour
- 1 teaspoon baking powder
- ½ teaspoon baking soda
- ¼ teaspoon salt
- ⅔ cup (4⅔ ounces) sugar
- 3 large eggs
- 3 tablespoons honey
- 2 tablespoons grated orange zest
- 1 tablespoon dried lavender (optional)
- ½ teaspoon vanilla extract

1. Adjust oven rack to middle position and heat oven to 350 degrees. Using ruler and pencil, draw two 13 by 2-inch rectangles, spaced 3 inches apart, on piece of parchment paper. Grease baking sheet and place parchment on it, marked side down.
2. Whisk flour, baking powder, baking soda, and salt together in small bowl. In large bowl, whisk sugar and eggs together until pale yellow. Whisk in honey, orange zest, lavender, if using, and vanilla until combined. Using rubber spatula, stir in flour mixture until just combined.
3. Divide dough in half. Using floured hands, form each half into 13 by 2-inch rectangle, using lines on parchment as guide. Using rubber spatula lightly coated with vegetable oil spray, smooth tops and sides of loaves. Bake until loaves are golden and just beginning to crack on top, about 35 minutes, rotating sheet halfway through baking.
4. Let loaves cool on sheet for 10 minutes, then transfer to cutting board. Reduce oven temperature to 325 degrees. Using serrated knife, slice each loaf on slight bias into ½-inch-thick slices.
5. Arrange cookies cut side down on sheet about ½ inch apart and bake until crisp and golden brown on both sides, about 15 minutes, flipping cookies halfway through baking. Let cool completely on wire rack before serving. (Biscotti can be stored at room temperature for up to 1 month.)

Eggs with Spinach & Nuts

Prep time: 5 minutes | Cook time: 25 minutes | Serves 4

- 1 lb spinach, rinsed, chopped
- 3 tbsp olive oil
- 1 tbsp butter
- 1 tbsp almonds, crushed
- 1 tbsp peanuts, crushed
- 4 eggs
- ½ tsp chili flakes
- ½ tsp sea salt

1. Pour 1 ½ cups of water into the inner pot and insert a steamer basket. Place the eggs onto the basket. Seal the lid and cook on High Pressure for 5 minutes.
2. Do a quick release. Remove the eggs to an ice bath. Wipe the pot clean, and heat oil on Sauté. Add spinach and cook for 2-3 minutes, stirring occasionally.
3. Stir in 1 tbsp of butter and season with salt and chili flakes. Mix well and cook for 1 more minute. Press Cancel and sprinkle with nuts. Peel and slice each egg in half, lengthwise. Transfer to a serving plate and pour over spinach mixture.

Olive Oil Ice Cream

Prep time: 5 minutes | Cook time: 25 minutes | Serves 8

- 4 large egg yolks
- ⅓ cup powdered sugar-free sweetener (such as stevia or monk fruit extract)
- 2 cups half-and-half or 1 cup heavy whipping cream and 1 cup whole milk
- 1 teaspoon vanilla extract
- ⅛ teaspoon salt
- ¼ cup light fruity extra-virgin olive oil

1. Freeze the bowl of an ice cream maker for at least 12 hours or overnight.
2. In a large bowl, whisk together the egg yolks and sugar-free sweetener.
3. In a small saucepan, heat the half-and-half over medium heat until just below a boil. Remove from the heat and allow to cool slightly.
4. Slowly pour the warm half-and-half into the egg mixture, whisking constantly to avoid cooking the eggs. Return the eggs and cream to the saucepan over low heat.
5. Whisking constantly, cook over low heat until thickened, 15 to 20 minutes. Remove from the heat and stir in the vanilla extract and salt. Whisk in the olive oil and transfer to a glass bowl. Allow to cool, cover, and refrigerate for at least 6 hours.
6. Freeze custard in an ice cream maker according to manufacturer's directions.

Appendix 1 Measurement Conversion Chart

Volume Equivalents (Dry)	
US STANDARD	METRIC (APPROXIMATE)
1/8 teaspoon	0.5 mL
1/4 teaspoon	1 mL
1/2 teaspoon	2 mL
3/4 teaspoon	4 mL
1 teaspoon	5 mL
1 tablespoon	15 mL
1/4 cup	59 mL
1/2 cup	118 mL
3/4 cup	177 mL
1 cup	235 mL
2 cups	475 mL
3 cups	700 mL
4 cups	1 L

Volume Equivalents (Liquid)		
US STANDARD	US STANDARD (OUNCES)	METRIC (APPROXIMATE)
2 tablespoons	1 fl.oz.	30 mL
1/4 cup	2 fl.oz.	60 mL
1/2 cup	4 fl.oz.	120 mL
1 cup	8 fl.oz.	240 mL
1 1/2 cup	12 fl.oz.	355 mL
2 cups or 1 pint	16 fl.oz.	475 mL
4 cups or 1 quart	32 fl.oz.	1 L
1 gallon	128 fl.oz.	4 L

Temperatures Equivalents	
FAHRENHEIT(F)	CELSIUS(C) APPROXIMATE)
225 °F	107 °C
250 °F	120 ° °C
275 °F	135 °C
300 °F	150 °C
325 °F	160 °C
350 °F	180 °C
375 °F	190 °C
400 °F	205 °C
425 °F	220 °C
450 °F	235 °C
475 °F	245 °C
500 °F	260 °C

Weight Equivalents	
US STANDARD	METRIC (APPROXIMATE)
1 ounce	28 g
2 ounces	57 g
5 ounces	142 g
10 ounces	284 g
15 ounces	425 g
16 ounces (1 pound)	455 g
1.5 pounds	680 g
2 pounds	907 g

Appendix 2 The Dirty Dozen and Clean Fifteen

The Environmental Working Group (EWG) is a nonprofit, nonpartisan organization dedicated to protecting human health and the environment Its mission is to empower people to live healthier lives in a healthier environment. This organization publishes an annual list of the twelve kinds of produce, in sequence, that have the highest amount of pesticide residue-the Dirty Dozen-as well as a list of the fifteen kinds ofproduce that have the least amount of pesticide residue-the Clean Fifteen.

THE DIRTY DOZEN

The 2016 Dirty Dozen includes the following produce. These are considered among the year's most important produce to buy organic:

Strawberries	Spinach
Apples	Tomatoes
Nectarines	Bell peppers
Peaches	Cherry tomatoes
Celery	Cucumbers
Grapes	Kale/collard greens
Cherries	Hot peppers

The Dirty Dozen list contains two additional itemskale/collard greens and hot peppers-because they tend to contain trace levels of highly hazardous pesticides.

THE CLEAN FIFTEEN

The least critical to buy organically are the Clean Fifteen list. The following are on the 2016 list:

Avocados	Papayas
Corn	Kiw
Pineapples	Eggplant
Cabbage	Honeydew
Sweet peas	Grapefruit
Onions	Cantaloupe
Asparagus	Cauliflower
Mangos	

Some of the sweet corn sold in the United States are made from genetically engineered (GE) seedstock. Buy organic varieties of these crops to avoid GE produce.

Appendix 3 Index

A

all-purpose flour 10, 16, 81, 84, 86
almond 18, 76, 79, 81, 85
anise seeds 84
apple 18, 26, 31, 42, 53, 74, 80, 83
asparagus 22, 26, 28, 77
avocado 12, 18, 20, 26, 65, 68, 84

B

bacon 44
baking powder 18, 79, 81, 84, 86
baking soda 10, 16, 39, 81, 86
balsamic vinegar 26, 32, 83, 86
basil 11, 15, 27, 29, 30, 36, 37, 40, 44, 61, 64
bell pepper 31, 35, 39, 65, 76
black beans 36
broccoli 13, 24, 31
butter 28, 30, 39, 40, 52, 53, 74, 79, 81, 83

C

carrot 26, 28, 30, 31, 37, 40, 53, 54, 62, 80
cauliflower 12, 17, 31, 72, 76
cayenne 26, 50, 53, 58, 75
cayenne pepper 26, 50, 53
cheese 11, 12, 13, 15, 16, 17, 19, 21, 22, 23
chicken 10, 15, 26, 34, 35, 38, 40, 42
chives 19, 40, 50, 74
cinnamon................. 10, 12, 16, 42, 45, 56, 59, 72, 79, 81, 84
cookies 81, 83, 84, 86
coriander 50, 56

corn 36, 89
cumin 45, 48, 50, 56, 58, 59, 72

D

Dijon mustard 63
dried dill 18, 80

E

egg 11, 12, 15, 20, 22, 24, 26, 31, 43, 50

F

flour 10, 11, 16, 18, 21, 23, 52, 53, 66, 69, 79, 81, 82
fresh chives 19, 40, 50, 74
fresh cilantro 22, 39, 48, 59, 65, 72, 75
fresh cilantro leaves 72
fresh dill 18
fresh parsley 10, 15, 17, 24, 31, 34, 35, 36
fresh parsley leaves 15, 53

G

garlic 10, 11, 12, 13, 15, 16, 17, 21, 22, 24, 27
garlic powder 27, 30, 43, 44, 45, 48, 53
Greek yogurt 18, 45, 47, 52, 67, 69, 72

H

honey 20, 21, 30, 54, 69, 74, 79, 86

J

juice 10, 11, 13, 15, 18, 21, 24, 26, 28

K

kale 11, 18, 26, 30, 34, 85
ketchup 58, 76
kosher salt 58, 61, 79

L

lemon juice 15, 18, 26, 30, 34, 37, 39, 43
lemon zest 13, 21, 24, 26, 43, 61
lime 64, 65

M

milk.................. 12, 13, 16, 17, 18, 20, 21, 24, 58, 71, 76, 81
Mozzarella 36
muffin 79
mustard 31, 48, 63, 65, 67, 68

N

nutmeg 10, 16, 80

O

olive oil 10, 11, 12, 13, 15, 16, 17, 18, 19, 20, 21
onion 11, 12, 13, 15, 20, 22, 24, 26, 27, 28, 31, 35
onion powder 58, 62, 64, 66
oregano 11, 13, 21, 28, 30, 32, 43, 45, 51

P

paprika 12, 24, 28, 38, 43, 44, 48
Parmesan cheese 15, 19, 21, 22, 23, 39, 73, 75, 85
parsley 10, 12, 15, 17, 23, 24, 26, 29, 31
potato 19, 20, 22, 27, 31, 50, 75

pumpkin 13, 81

R

red pepper flakes 10, 13, 24, 37, 42, 55, 61, 82
rice 17, 34, 35, 36, 37, 38, 39, 40
ricotta cheese 13, 17, 71, 81, 85

S

saffron 35, 71
salt 10, 11, 12, 13, 15, 16, 17, 19, 20, 21
sauce 21, 36, 37, 40, 44, 45, 46, 47, 51
sugar 10, 11, 13, 16, 17, 18, 21, 23, 36

T

tahini 80
thyme 24, 30, 35, 42, 43, 44, 58, 63, 64, 67, 68

U

unsalted butter 28, 30, 39, 40, 52, 53, 74, 79, 81, 83

V

vinegar 10, 12, 16, 42, 45, 56, 59

W

white wine 81, 83, 84, 86
wine vinegar 19, 40, 50, 74

Y

yogurt 18, 45, 47, 52, 67, 69, 72

Z

zucchini 15, 28, 72, 73

The Mediterranean Diet Cookbook for Beginners | 91

Sandra H. Herrington

Printed in Great Britain
by Amazon